VICTORIA BENEDICTS

Victoria Benedictsson was born as Victoria Maria Bruzelius in rural Sweden in 1850. She was brought up by her father and received an extensive education, which was at that time reserved mainly for boys. When she was twenty-one, she married the widower Christian Benedictsson, who brought with him five children from his previous marriage.

She is known mainly for her novels dealing with social issues as well as a number of stories about country life and other novels dealing with social issues. Her play, *The Enchantment* (written in 1888), was only discovered and published after her death and not performed until 1910.

Following the success of her novel *Money* (published under a male pseudonym), Victoria Benedictsson moved to Stockholm, where she quickly became involved in literary circles, befriending Ibsen and Strindberg, who supposedly based the character of Miss Julie on her. At that time she also met the literary critic Georg Brandes, with whom she embarked on a scandalous and very public affair. Following his rejection of her as a lover, and, more importantly, a writer (he refused to review her novel), she committed suicide in 1888.

CLARE BAYLEY

Clare Bayley developed her version of *The Enchantment* while on attachment at the National Theatre Studio.

Her other plays include *The Container*, which premiered at the 2007 Edinburgh Festival; *The Woman Who Swallowed a Pin* (Southwark Playhouse); *The Shift* and *Blavatsky* (both Young Vic Studio); and *Northern Lights* (also produced on radio).

For radio her work includes *The Bringer of Sweets* (BBC/CBL). She was awarded the Sunday Times Screenwriting award for the screenplay *Corridors in the Air*.

Her publications include *Guatemala Moon* (Serpent's Tail) and *The Container* (Nick Hern Books).

Victoria Benedictsson

THE
ENCHANTMENT

in a new version by

CLARE BAYLEY

from a literal translation by
Ben Anderman

NICK HERN BOOKS

London

www.nickhernbooks.co.uk

A Nick Hern Book

The Enchantment first published in Great Britain in 2007 as a
paperback original by Nick Hern Books Limited, 14 Larden Road,
London W3 7ST

This version of *The Enchantment* copyright © 2007 by Clare Bayley
Introduction copyright © 2007 by Clare Bayley

This version is from a literal translation by Ben Anderman

Clare Bayley has asserted her moral right to be identified as
the author of this work

Cover image: © istockphoto.com/milosluzanin
Cover design: Ned Hoste, 2H

Typeset by Country Setting, Kingsdown, Kent CT14 8ES
Printed and bound in Great Britain by CPI Cox & Wyman, Reading,
Berks RG1 8EX

A CIP catalogue record for this book is available from the British
Library

ISBN 978 1 85459 999 5

Love, Literature and the Arbiters of Taste

'It gave her confidence, which for a writer is the most important thing,' says Gustave Alland in Act I of *The Enchantment*. Victoria Benedictsson's confidence as a writer was secured in 1885 with the publication of her novel *Money (Pengar)*. Until then she had written short stories of life in the rural southern province of Skane, where she lived. But after a riding accident left her bedbound for virtually two years, she produced the novel which secured her reputation as a writer.

Money was published under the male pseudonym of Ernst Ahlgren because its frank treatment of relationships between men and women would have been considered scandalous for a woman to write. It was clearly a response to Ibsen's *A Doll's House*, which had been performed and published six years earlier. But *Money* pushed the debate about women and marriage a little further. Its heroine, Selma, was neither neurotic nor infantilised, and resisted the temptations of adultery with great strength of character. The root of her malaise was nothing of her doing, but unequivocally depicted by her status as chattel, bought by her husband from her father. *Money* remains Benedictsson's most famous work and is studied by students of literature in every Swedish university.

On the strength of its success at the time, Benedictsson moved to Stockholm. This was a bold step for a thirty-five-year-old married woman. She was leaving behind a husband, Christian, whom she had married at the age of twenty-one. He was twenty-eight years her senior, and when they married he already had five children. Together they had two further daughters, Ellen, who survived for less than a month, and Hilma.

In Stockholm Benedictsson quickly left her provincial life behind, and was enthusiastically taken up in literary circles. It perhaps came naturally to her. Like Hedda Gabler, she had been brought up as a son by her father, who gave her the education that would normally have been reserved for boys. As a young woman, she hoped to go to art school, but instead was married off. Ferociously intelligent and learned, her life as a provincial wife and mother was never going to be a fulfilling one.

Stockholm at the time was a ferment of cultural and intellectual activity. The Modern Breakthrough was underway – a movement which placed the social and political issues of the day at the centre of artistic endeavour. Naturalism and realism were the radical new forms, and the condition of women in society was one of its central subjects.

The Modern Breakthrough had largely come about due to the influence of the Danish critic and scholar, Georg Brandes. At the age of thirty, Brandes formulated the principles of this new realism, and in 1871 gave a series of public lectures berating the people of Denmark for being forty years behind the rest of Europe. The lectures were a sensation. But despite his popularity and the impact he had on cultural life in Scandinavia, Brandes was considered dangerously radical. He was denied a professorship which was widely assumed to be his for the taking. In retreat, he travelled in Europe – to England, Italy and France before settling in Berlin for five years.

He used this time of exile to collect up the work of many European writers, which he then introduced to the Scandinavian public: they included Nietzsche, Voltaire and J.S. Mill, whose *The Subjection of Women* he translated in 1869.

Brandes also took up the cause of contemporary Scandinavian writers. He championed Søren Kierkegaard, and even introduced Nietzsche to his work. And he befriended the emerging naturalist dramatists of the time, particularly Ibsen, Strindberg and Bjørnstjerne Bjørnson.

By the time he returned to Copenhagen in 1883, he was hailed as the father of the Modern Breakthrough and the ultimate arbiter of literary taste. It was probably inevitable that Brandes and Benedictsson should meet. Benedictsson was at the hub of cultural life in Stockholm and often visited Copenhagen. She knew Ibsen and Strindberg – it is said that Strindberg based the character of Miss Julie on her, and that Ibsen's character of Hedda Gabler was influenced by her.

Brandes and Benedictsson embarked on a high-profile love affair. Initially Benedictsson fought to keep it on a platonic basis, but it soon developed into a fully sexual liaison. The affair has captured the imagination of succeeding generations and has almost overshadowed Benedictsson's reputation as a writer. It has inspired countless plays, stories, novels and filmscripts. But the most compelling and fascinating account of the affair is Benedictsson's own, in her play *The Enchantment*.

With unstinting clarity, devastating honesty and forensic detail, she plots the course of this ill-fated passion. Her style of writing is fresh, bold and truly original. Though reminiscent of Ibsen, Strindberg, even Chekhov, it is something completely of its own.

But one crucial aspect of the story is missing from the play. Louise, unlike Victoria, is not an artist or a writer. Indeed, when Alland asks her, she claims to have no interest or activity at all, not even needlework. She envies Mr Moller his engrossing work as a bank manager. She longs for 'Numbers lined up in rows on paper, crowding into your head and blocking out all other thoughts'. When Erna is broken-hearted, she is able to throw her energies into her work, and survives personal devastation by turning it into artistic success. But this avenue of escape is denied to Louise.

This strange omission is profoundly significant. Benedictsson was in love with Brandes, the supreme critic and writer of the day, and she considered herself his equal. She was at the height of her powers as a writer. And she had a burning subject which she wanted to write about.

Benedictsson had a utopian vision of marriage as an equal sharing of work and responsibility between men and women. She never believed that women's sexual emancipation should lead to free love, any more than she believed that a married woman should become the property of her husband. For its time, this view was radical and deeply unfashionable. But no doubt she saw her relationship with Brandes as the prototype of this ideal.

During the time that she was with Brandes, she wrote a defining novel to propound this view and prove its validity. With Brandes beside her, it was not unreasonable for her to assume that both her work and her views would be taken up in the cultural

debate and that her place at the centre of intellectual life would
be further secured.

This novel was *Fru Marianne* (*Mrs Marianne*), and it was
published in 1887. To her shock and devastation, Brandes
disdained to review it. During thirty years as a critic, he never
once reviewed the work of a female author. Instead, he passed
his lover's novel to his younger brother Edvard, who dismissed
it as 'too much of a ladies' novel'. It is an accusation against
the work of women writers which is still familiar today, and
whose sting is no less poisonous now than it was in 1887.
From time to time a row blows up, and accusations fly. But it
rarely changes the proportion of plays written or directed by
women that are produced on our stages.

Benedictsson did not have the resources to overcome such a
brutal rejection. In one blow Brandes had destroyed her
confidence, which she clearly considered to be 'the most
important thing'. He had rejected her both as a lover and as
a writer. Never the most robust of characters, Benedictsson
described this double attack as her 'death sentence'.

She wrote *The Enchantment* (*Den Bergtagna*) in 1888, choosing
to make its central character, Louise, a woman with no artistic
vocation or talent. On July 21 of that year, Benedictsson checked
into a hotel room in Copenhagen and killed herself by cutting
her own throat.

By doing this, she all but wrote herself out of history. While
Ibsen's output spans almost half a century, Benedictsson had
only a few years. Her oeuvre remains small. Outside of Sweden,
she is almost completely unknown. But her writing speaks to
readers and audiences now, perhaps even more than it did then.

The Enchantment was discovered after her death by her
favourite stepdaughter Matti, who passed it to Benedictsson's
friend, the writer Axel Lundegård. He completed and published
it posthumously. It was given six performances at Svenska
Teatern in Stockholm in May 1910. The production at the
National Theatre in 2007, for which this version was prepared,
was its British premiere.

Clare Bayley

The Enchantment was first performed in the Cottesloe auditorium of the National Theatre, London, on 1 August 2007, with previews from 24 July 2007, with the following cast:

LOUISE STRANDBERG	Nancy Carroll
ERNA WALLDEN	Niamh Cusack
HENRIK RYBERG	Edward Davenport
VIGGO PIHL	Hugh Skinner
GUSTAVE ALLAND	Zubin Varla
LILLY WALLDEN	Claudia Renton
THE CONCIERGE	Avril Elgar
BOTILDA	Marlene Sidaway
MRS KNUTSON	Judith Coke
MISS KNUTSON	Madeleine Herrington
MR MOLLER	Patrick Drury
THE POSTMAN	Ray Newe

Director Paul Miller
Designer Simon Daw
Lighting Designer Bruno Poet
Sound Designer John Leonard
Music David Shrubsole

THE ENCHANTMENT

*For my father
an enchanter*

C.B.

Characters
in order of appearance

LOUISE STRANDBERG

ERNA WALLDEN

HENRIK RYBERG

VIGGO PIHL

GUSTAVE ALLAND

LILLY WALLDEN, *Erna's sister*

CONCIERGE

BOTILDA, *Louise's nanny/housekeeper*

MRS KNUTSON

MISS KNUTSON

THE POSTMAN

MR MOLLER, *the Bank Manager*

ACT ONE

A sunny May day in Paris.

A basement studio. French windows open onto a courtyard garden, enclosed by a high wall. There's ivy on the walls and a cherry tree in blossom.

The room is sparsely furnished with a chaise longue, a table, an antique cabinet and a few chairs. On the walls are scattered sketches which have been left behind by a previous occupant.

On the right is a door to the hall; on the left, a door to the bedroom. There is an iron stove near the bedroom door.

LOUISE *is lying on the chaise longue, propped up by pillows and with a blanket over her feet.*

HENRIK *is sitting in front of the stove, smoking a pipe.*

ERNA *is making tea at the stove. As she goes to the cabinet to get cups etc., she picks up a corner of the blanket that has fallen on the floor.*

LOUISE. Thank you, Erna. The worst thing about being ill is all the trouble you cause to everyone else.

ERNA. I'm only making you a cup of tea. If that's what you call trouble, then you really have led a very sheltered life.

LOUISE. I don't just mean today. I mean over the last few months.

ERNA. There's nothing to be said. It's all over now, anyway. In a couple of days you'll be completely fine, you'll be up and about. Won't you? (*To* HENRIK, *as she passes*.) Can I have a go on your pipe?

HENRIK. No.

ERNA. Just a little puff?

HENRIK. No. It's mine. I'm enjoying it.

ERNA (*to* LOUISE). Do you have any biscuits, Lou?

LOUISE. Yes – there's a tin somewhere.

> LOUISE *takes the cup*. ERNA *gets the biscuits*.

ERNA (*sitting on the edge of the chaise longue*). Here – lovely.

> *They eat biscuits*.

> That's better, isn't it?

LOUISE. Yes.

ERNA. You're a little Paleface today.

LOUISE. And you're an Amazon. Every day.

ERNA (*to* HENRIK). I suppose you'll be wanting one too?

HENRIK. No. Thank you.

ERNA. Oh, go on! Don't be like that.

HENRIK. I said no!

ERNA (*bending down as if to a naughty child*). You are moody today. I suppose you want me to make you some coffee?

HENRIK. I don't want anything! Leave me alone.

ERNA. Ow! The spikes are out. What a Hedgehog! (*To* LOUISE.) Where have Lilly and Viggo got to?

LOUISE. I should think they can look after themselves. Don't fuss.

ERNA. Don't fuss, she says! But I know the pitfalls that await her.

LOUISE. You can trust Viggo to look after her.

ERNA. Yes. I suppose I can.

LOUISE. You sound more like a mother than a sister.

ERNA. I'm twelve years wiser than she is. And I'm responsible for her while she's here in Paris.

LOUISE. I really don't think you need to worry.

ERNA. It's better than letting her run wild.

Now – more tea?

LOUISE. Is there enough? You haven't had yours yet.

ERNA. I only need to fill up the pot. Since Hedgehog here doesn't want any.

You're dozing off over that pipe! Go on – let me have a little puff. You're so mean!

HENRIK. No.

ERNA. Not even one puff?

HENRIK. No.

ERNA. God! What strength of character.

She pours more tea and sits again on the edge of the chaise longue.

I know what you're thinking. (*Suddenly speaking low and urgently.*) I'm not going to let her fall into the same traps that I fell into.

LOUISE. You were quite happy to fall into them. Why deny the same pleasure to your little sister?

ERNA. You can be so naive sometimes. Happy?

LOUISE. Do you mean you're not happy?

ERNA. Well, I suppose you can survive almost anything. That's what's so damnable.

LOUISE. You don't regret it, do you? You always *seem* happy.

ERNA. It's essential to keep up a brave face. Besides – there are always consolations. (*She looks over at* HENRIK.) There's always a pipeful of tobacco, isn't there, Henrik?

Or not.

She begins pacing.

It is odd that they're not back yet.

HENRIK. You've been to visit Bergstrøm, haven't you?

ERNA. Yes.

HENRIK. And you took him flowers! How *charming*. How very genteel.

ERNA. Yes, indeed.

HENRIK. When did you last bring me flowers?

ERNA. Have you broken your leg?

HENRIK. Oh – I see. You only took him flowers because of his leg. Of course!

ERNA. Of course not. Not *only* because of his leg. Because of the rest of him, too. Because if he was here now I wouldn't be standing here longing for a bit of a smoke.

HENRIK. Ah! So you actually admit –

ERNA. My darling, my Adonis, I would shower you with flowers. I would fulfil your every desire. If only you were a bit less grumpy!

HENRIK. I don't want your flowers.

ERNA (*humming, she walks up to* LOUISE). I wouldn't have let Lilly come if I hadn't felt I had to. She begged and implored me in every letter she wrote. I just couldn't say no. And it won't do her any harm to learn to speak French properly. *N'est-ce pas*?

LOUISE. But Erna – what's so dangerous about coming to Paris?

ERNA. Life out here in the wild with us artists is hardly the best preparation for a nice, respectable gal destined for a life of tedious gentility back home. Here the leash is loosened a little – and there are some peculiar specimens to be found in the art world.

HENRIK. You are one of the most peculiar of the lot.

ERNA. Do you think so?

HENRIK. Do you really think I haven't noticed how you're trying to charm him?

ERNA. Am I not trying to charm you, too?

Please let me borrow your pipe.

HENRIK. I can't *stand* it any more. You're driving me insane with all your carryings on.

ERNA. Fine. So leave. You can, you know.

HENRIK. That's what you want, isn't it?

ERNA. I don't want it. I don't fear it, either. But if your jealousy is going to drive both of us mad, I think it's best we go our separate ways.

HENRIK. Here we go again – more threats! One day you'll push me too far.

ERNA. How far is too far?

LOUISE. Calm down, you two – please.

ERNA. His pettiness is driving me mad.

HENRIK. If you weren't so secretive –

ERNA. I am not secretive! I'm nice to my friends! Bergstrom is my friend. If ever he becomes more than a friend, I promise you will be the first to know.

HENRIK. So it *is* a possibility?

ERNA. I've lived long enough to learn not to rule out any possibility.

HENRIK. Yes – and you've really *lived*, haven't you? You've been about a bit. But I don't know any of that. I don't even know how many –

ERNA. Stop there, or we'll pass the point of no return.

You know I've already told you about the one, and the only one, whom I will not mention.

HENRIK. That's what's so intolerable! I might meet him on the street! I might be coming around a corner and bump right into him. I might have done that already, I can't tell. So I suspect everyone! It's hell!

ERNA. You'll never meet him.

HENRIK. How can you say that?

ERNA. I told you. It's as if he's dead.

HENRIK. *As if* he's dead! So he's *not* dead!

LOUISE. Ah – Lilly and Viggo are back.

ERNA (*to* HENRIK). Don't say another word! Not one word
in case she hears.

VIGGO *enters, carrying a bunch of flowers.*

(*Vehemently.*) Where's Lilly?

VIGGO. She'll be here soon. (*He gives the flowers to*
LOUISE.) I brought a breath of summer for our invalid.

LOUISE. Thank you. You're all so kind.

ERNA (*to* HENRIK). There – you see! Viggo brings flowers to
someone who's laid up, and no one bats an eyelid!

VIGGO. Lilly went to Maison Blanche to buy something I'm
not supposed to know about. I thought she'd be here by
now. I stopped off at the Café de la Regence to have a look
at the papers, and – (*To* LOUISE.) consequently I've got a
surprise for you.

LOUISE. A newspaper?

VIGGO. No. A person. Can you guess?

LOUISE. Pelle?

VIGGO. Pelle! No. Somebody significant. A famous artist.

LOUISE. In this city, that could be anyone – famous artists are
two a penny.

VIGGO. This one is different. He's someone you admire.

LOUISE. Not Alland? Gustave Alland?

VIGGO *nods.*

The Gustave Alland?

VIGGO. Absolutely.

LOUISE. Is he here, in Paris?

VIGGO. Yes – after two years away.

LOUISE. Why has he been away?

ERNA. He'd ground to a halt, artistically, while others raced ahead. He retreated with his tail between his legs.

LOUISE. In whose opinion did he 'grind to a halt'?

ERNA. His last show wasn't up to much. And he hasn't exhibited since.

VIGGO. There were a couple of busts at the salon.

ERNA. Ah yes – busts of minor royals.

VIGGO. Royals are humans, too.

ERNA *laughs scornfully.*

LOUISE. What's he like?

VIGGO. You'll find out in a minute.

ERNA *and* LOUISE. What?

VIGGO. He's coming here.

LOUISE. Here? Why?

VIGGO. To meet you, of course. That's the surprise!

ERNA (*through clenched teeth*). You dear, sweet man.

LOUISE. When?

VIGGO. Now! Any minute.

LOUISE. I'll have to get dressed.

VIGGO. No – I told him you were ill.

ERNA. I'm off, then.

LOUISE. Are you going?

ERNA. You know I can't stand geniuses.

LOUISE. You've got to stay and help me out! What am I going to talk about? What am I going to do?

ERNA. Toodle-oo.

VIGGO. Look at her! I only did it to cheer her up, and it's put her into a complete frenzy!

ERNA. Sweet Bumpkin. Make sure you're better by tomorrow.

LOUISE. Aren't you going to look in on me tonight?

ERNA. Yes – probably.

She kisses LOUISE *on the head.*

(*To* HENRIK.) Come on, Hedgehog.

HENRIK *gets up unhurriedly and knocks out his pipe. They leave.*

LOUISE. I'm so nervous.

VIGGO. Don't be. He's only a sculptor.

LOUISE. If I start to gabble, just kick me and change the subject.

VIGGO. I'm not staying.

LOUISE. What?!

VIGGO. I've got to pack.

LOUISE. I will miss you, Viggo. You've been so good to me.

VIGGO. I'll miss you too. I'm not looking forward to going back.

LOUISE. You mean you'll miss Lilly.

VIGGO. Everything here. But maybe her most of all.

LOUISE. Thank you for everything you've done for me.

VIGGO. It wasn't much.

LOUISE. You've looked after me – you've been like a mother to me all this time. You and Erna.

VIGGO (*smiles*). That's another reason why I'm loath to leave. My patient might need me.

LOUISE. I'm sure I'll stop being such a malingerer once you're not around to indulge me.

VIGGO. You're not a malingerer. You're delicate. You haven't got such thick skin as the rest of us.

LOUISE. I'm going back soon, too. Will you come and visit me, in the summer?

VIGGO. Yes – I will. Let's shake on it. (*They shake.*) Goodbye.

LOUISE. Please, can't you just wait until Alland comes? What on earth am I going to talk to him about?

VIGGO. Just be yourself – that's all you need to do. (*There's a knock at the door.*) *Ah!* Come in!

ALLAND *enters*.

There you are. My patient was just telling me her powers of conversation are quite weakened.

LOUISE *sits up*.

ALLAND. No – don't move. I hear you've been very unwell.

LOUISE. I'm very honoured that you should come and visit.

ALLAND (*to* VIGGO). I see Miss Strandberg's illness has not, however, affected her ability to be charming.

Are you off? I hope I'm not scaring you away?

VIGGO. Not at all. But I'm catching the evening train and I haven't even packed yet.

ALLAND. Will you be away for long?

VIGGO. I think so.

ALLAND. You'll be much missed by your stepsister, I'm sure. Isn't that right? You're Mr Pihl's stepsister?

LOUISE. Yes.

ALLAND. I imagine you'll be quite lonely without him.

LOUISE. Very much so.

VIGGO *nods to* LOUISE, *bows to* ALLAND *and leaves*.

ALLAND. Do you want to lie back down?

LOUISE. No – I'm fine. I can sit up.

ALLAND. Let me look at you.

LOUISE. Not very inspiring, I'm afraid.

ALLAND. You've wasted away.

LOUISE. I've had typhoid.

ALLAND (*scrutinising her face with a professional eye*). The angles – the shadows . . . and the eyes! I like you. You have very honest eyes.

LOUISE *smiles*.

(*Irritably.*) I didn't mean to flatter you.

LOUISE. No – I didn't –

ALLAND. It's irrelevant to me whether you're ugly or beautiful. It's a purely professional interest.

LOUISE. Do you know my brother's work?

ALLAND. Yes. He's very talented. He's as good as he's cracked up to be. Which is rare. Ah – now your face is lighting up. I see you're proud of him. I expect he's livened up your life a bit.

LOUISE. Yes. We're very close. When we were growing up, he always came home for the summer. And when he was away he'd write.

ALLAND. And now?

LOUISE. He's about to be married.

ALLAND. Ah! That's the ruination of most of us.

LOUISE. That's not what I meant.

ALLAND. No, but it's true. But you were saying? When you were growing up . . .

LOUISE. There's not much to tell.

ALLAND. Oh, I'm sure there is. I can read it in your face. You have a haunted look about you.

LOUISE *hides her face with her hands.*

I'd guess that life has dealt you some blows.

LOUISE. You could say that. My father died when I was seventeen. Then my sister had a breakdown. And my mother fell ill. I couldn't care for both of them, so my sister had to be sent to an asylum. Soon after that, my mother died. At that point, my doctor said a change of scenery might do me good.

ALLAND. And this is your first time away from home?

LOUISE. Yes.

ALLAND. It must have been a dizzy moment, flying the nest for the first time.

LOUISE. I fell ill almost immediately.

ALLAND. I'm sorry.

Is this your brother's studio?

LOUISE. He'd taken it on for a year, and then since it was empty he thought I might as well move in.

ALLAND. It's lovely and spacious. And you have a garden.

But don't you get lonely here, in this big room, all on your own?

LOUISE. I have a little bedroom, through there – and I'm not on my own. I have compatriots in the building – Erna Wallden, the painter, lives just upstairs.

ALLAND. She lives here?

LOUISE. Do you know her?

ALLAND. I've met her – it was some time ago now.

LOUISE. She's been so good to me. She's really taken care of me – she's done everything.

ALLAND. High praise! I never realised Mademoiselle Wallden was such a ministering angel.

LOUISE. She seems tough, but inside she *is* angelic.

ALLAND. You have the most enormous eyes! You're not at all like your brother.

LOUISE. No. (*She lowers her eyes.*)

ALLAND (*imitating her*). Why did you do that?

LOUISE (*timidly*). You were looking at me – rather oddly.

ALLAND (*laughs*). I was looking at you honestly! (*More seriously.*) You're just like someone I used to know.

LOUISE. That explains it, then.

ALLAND. It doesn't need to be explained. Looking is what I do. For me it's the same as breathing. I look – and I see. And from every face I look at – I learn something.

A pause.

LOUISE. Who was she – the one you think I'm like?

ALLAND. Someone very close to me.

LOUISE. I'm so sorry –

ALLAND (*quickly*). No harm done – neither to you, nor to me.

Are you a painter?

LOUISE. No.

ALLAND. Do you have any kind of work – I don't mean lace-making or needlework. I mean – some kind of vocation?

LOUISE. No.

ALLAND. Ah well. That just leaves marriage, then.

LOUISE (*smiling*). The ruination of us all?

ALLAND. That's how it goes – a woman must marry, or she'll wither on the vine. A great pity, in your case.

LOUISE. Do you think so?

ALLAND. Yes. I'm sure you could make a man – as they say – very happy.

You're a 'good' person, aren't you?

LOUISE (*cheerfully*). Yes, unfortunately.

ALLAND. You've noticed it too, then. All this preaching about being good is nothing but self-interest. Because good people are always trampled underfoot. Remember that! You're much better off killing someone than loving her.

LOUISE. That's horrible. Don't say that.

ALLAND. It's how things are.

LOUISE. Don't you believe in love?

ALLAND. Oh yes – but I don't believe in women. Not many of them are equal to being loved.

LOUISE. What do you mean by that?

ALLAND. I mean that they can't cope with the way men are. With the way, for us, love is no more than an episode in your life.

LOUISE. If that's the case then it's a credit to our sex.

ALLAND. Are you sure? I remember someone – a painter, I think. For two years she lived with a friend of mine. He was a painter, too, and they helped and supported each other in their work. But she was younger, and less well-known as an artist. It ended as it always ends.

LOUISE. How?

ALLAND. Love is nothing but a flame which flares up – and dies back. Bright, but brief. My friend and his lover parted. They both got tired of each other.

LOUISE. Did she get tired of him?

ALLAND. Does that alarm you? Yes, she did! But she hated him afterwards – as women always do when they stop loving.

LOUISE. Always?

ALLAND. That's where your sex let themselves down. A man always retains some affection for a woman he has loved. But women never do.

LOUISE. You can't generalise like that.

But what happened to her – the painter?

ALLAND. She's doing very nicely, thank you! While she was with him she painted a self-portrait. It was a masterpiece – bold, uncompromising, true. It was exhibited, it won all sorts of prizes, and then it was bought for the national collection. It launched her career – and what's more, it gave her confidence, which for an artist is the most important thing.

LOUISE. And then?

ALLAND. She has a show every year. Her paintings are so good that if you didn't know better, you'd swear they were done by a man.

LOUISE. I didn't mean her work. I meant what happened to her . . . inside.

ALLAND. That's why her work is so powerful. I'd say you could sum it up in two words: *she hates*. Love was no more than a brief moment, but the fire of it forged her into a true artist.

LOUISE. Poor woman!

ALLAND. No! You wouldn't say that if you knew what it is to produce great work.

But it's time I was going. (*Suddenly turning.*) Why did you say 'poor woman'? While they were together they both produced their best work. He did too.

LOUISE. Because of her?

ALLAND. Who knows? For me, every love affair brings a new work of art.

LOUISE. Really? So how have the last couple of years been for you?

ALLAND (*smiling*). Just a few busts, I'm afraid. (*He bows goodbye.*) How long will you be staying in Paris?

LOUISE. The studio is rented until July.

ALLAND. That gives you just over a month. And your garden is charming – wild and secret. You're nicely hidden away from the world here.

LOUISE. Do you like it?

ALLAND. I like everything I see here. It could be so lovely. But you're a Spartan. I can see it in your dress, and in the way you do your hair – so stern!

And in your heart of hearts, what's your judgement on me? Is it a sin to enjoy life?

When the sun shines, do you hide under a parasol and creep off into the shade? Not me. I would roll around in the grass when the sun is at its hottest.

You think I'm shallow, don't you?

LOUISE *shrugs*.

LOUISE. No. But it feels as if the world you live in is not the same as the world I live in.

LILLY *enters, running. She stops, embarrassed, when she sees* ALLAND.

Mademoiselle Wallden – Monsieur Gustave Alland.

LILLY *greets him*.

LILLY. Has Viggo left already?

LOUISE. Yes – he had to go and pack.

LILLY. Oh no!

LOUISE. You've been out for quite some time –

LILLY. I went past such a beautiful wedding at the Madeleine – I just had to stop and watch, and I forgot the time.

ALLAND (*with obvious interest in* LILLY). Don't worry, Mademoiselle Wallden. I'm sure he'll be back.

LILLY. Do you think so?

ALLAND. The more I look at you, the more likely it seems.

ERNA (*from the hall*). Lilly! Is Lilly in there?

LILLY. I'm just coming!

ALLAND (*bows*). I hope I will see you in good health again very soon. (*He takes* LOUISE's *hand*.) What a lovely hand. A fragile, bloodless little thing, yet exquisitely crafted.

He kisses it. LOUISE *pulls her hand away.*

Why did you do that? What's wrong with the men in your country? Don't they kiss ladies' hands?

LOUISE. Yes, but –

ALLAND. I'll always kiss a lady's hand – so long as it's beautiful.

LILLY *has taken off her glove and is studying her hand.*

Goodbye, Mademoiselle Wallden.

ALLAND *is about to leave when* ERNA *enters. She sees him, steps aside and stares at him fixedly. He bows quickly and exits.*

LOUISE. Is everything all right?

ERNA. Yes, of course. I just got a bit of a fright – I thought Monsieur Alland had already left, and then there he was lurking behind the door. (*She attempts to laugh.*) I think it must be the Hedgehog up there making me all frazzled with his nagging. (*To* LILLY.) Why didn't you come straight up?

LILLY. I thought Viggo would still be here.

ERNA. Viggo, Viggo, Viggo! I don't want you chasing after him all over the place like that.

LILLY. But you said yourself –

LOUISE. What is it, Erna? You're all of a jitter.

ERNA. I am on edge. All my nerves are jangling about.

LOUISE *leads her to the chaise longue and sits her down.*

LOUISE. Sit down. You poor old Amazon.

ERNA. I'll be all right. (*She jumps up again.*) Lilly – have you said your goodbyes?

LILLY. To whom?

ERNA. To whom? To your one and only, of course.

LILLY. No, I haven't.

ERNA. So I suppose he'll be back in a minute.

LILLY. I don't know!

ERNA. Of course he will.

LOUISE. Are you finding it hard – him going away?

LILLY. My life will be so empty, so horribly empty.

    LOUISE *kisses* LILLY's *forehead*.

ACT TWO

A June day in Paris.

The same studio, but with more furniture, curtains in front of the windows and a few large Japanese lanterns hanging from the ceiling. On the table, a vase full of roses. On a smaller table next to the chaise longue, a portrait of ALLAND.

LOUISE, *now in an elegant new Parisian outfit, greets the* CONCIERGE, *who has just entered.*

CONCIERGE. It's the twenty-second of June, and on the first of July the lease –

LOUISE. I'll take it for an extra month.

Two months.

All right, three months, if necessary.

CONCIERGE. I can't let it for less than a year, as I told you just the other day.

LOUISE. Six months, then. I'll take it for six months.

CONCIERGE. It's twelve months or nothing. The new tenant is waiting for an answer, and he can put his money on the table. On the table!

LOUISE. So can I.

CONCIERGE. Then you have first refusal.

LOUISE. I can pay half now, and the rest on the first of September. I don't have it all right now.

CONCIERGE. I can wait until September. But you'll give me something for the little extras, won't you?

LOUISE. If you'll let me arrange things as I've asked –

CONCIERGE. I am discretion personified. I've been about a bit myself, you know. I'm not some clodhopping provincial oaf, as I'm sure you'll appreciate.

LOUISE (*impatiently*). Yes. Yes –

CONCIERGE. Good. It suits me to have you here – that's why I'm letting you stay on. And Monsieur Alland, too – such a distinguished gent. Such manners!

LOUISE goes to the cabinet and starts to count out the money.

If there's anything else you want me to do – pick up some groceries for you, anything like that – I'm at your service.

LOUISE (*handing her the money*). Here. I think you'll find that's right.

CONCIERGE. Very good. I'll give you a receipt – and then, of course, there's the furniture. All this furniture that your brother rented, that'll be available too, from the first of July.

LOUISE. Perhaps we can discuss that later.

CONCIERGE. Very well. You can have everything just how you want it.

She leaves.

LOUISE. God – I'm mad. I'm mad! But I can't help it.

The CONCIERGE *re-enters.*

CONCIERGE. They're here again – the painter and her sister. Shall I – ?

LOUISE. Please show them in.

CONCIERGE. If you say so. I'm only thinking of what's best for you. I'd never let anyone in without first telling them that you're out.

LOUISE (*distracted*). Yes, yes!

CONCIERGE. I do it out of friendship – Lord knows, out of pure friendship for you and the handsome gentleman. Don't get me wrong, of course, but I was young once, you know – not that you'd know it now! And I remember what it was like – oh yes, I certainly remember what it was like –

She exits at a trot.

LOUISE (*to herself*). Oh Christ, where is he? What have I done wrong? Why doesn't he come?

ERNA and LILLY enter.

ERNA. The postman has brought some good news.

She hands LOUISE an opened letter. LOUISE reads distractedly.

LOUISE. I don't quite . . .

ERNA. Don't you understand? I've been awarded an artist's bursary.

LILLY (*delighted*). Nine thousand crowns. Well, that is three thousand each year for three years.

LOUISE (*faintly*). Well done, Erna.

LILLY. And that means, I can stay on!

ERNA. That's not what I said.

LILLY. You wouldn't have the heart to send me back.

LOUISE. I'm staying on, too – for a while at least.

ERNA. But I thought you couldn't afford to?

LOUISE. I think I can get by for a bit longer.

LILLY. That's the spirit! You've got money, after all. You just have to have a word with that bank manager of yours back home. I'm so happy! We'll have so much fun!

ERNA (*gruffly*). Oh – will we? Louise has retreated so far into her own little world that we barely see her any more.

LILLY (*with her arm around LOUISE's waist*). Yes, but now we're going to haul her back out again!

LOUISE. Don't say that!

ERNA. These days you always seem to be out when your friends come to call.

She sees the portrait of ALLAND and is momentarily unnerved.

LOUISE. I go to the theatre quite often – and then there are my French lessons.

ERNA (*looking at the portrait*). Who exactly is your French teacher?

There's an embarrassed silence.

LILLY. Guess what! I've had a letter from Viggo.

LOUISE (*coolly*). Really?

ERNA. Sixteen pages of nonsense.

LILLY goes to the window and starts reading.

It's looking very different around here! Lots of new stuff in the old place. You're spending like there's no tomorrow, aren't you? Oh – don't take it the wrong way. You know I can't help mothering everyone.

LOUISE turns away.

Are you annoyed?

LOUISE. No.

ERNA. I suppose it's none of my business, what you get up to.

Look at that – she's reading her letter again! That's the fourth time.

LILLY. It's not. I just wanted to check something.

ERNA. Yes – and you're 'just checking' every single one of its sixteen pages.

LILLY. Oh, shush! I wanted to tell Louise that Viggo has managed to find a publisher for his short stories, and he thinks he'll be able to get a permanent job as Paris correspondent here, and –

ERNA. And . . . and . . . and . . . ! We all have such high hopes for things that never happen in the end.

LILLY. You're in a bristly old mood today.

ERNA. I'm sorry. No one can be like velvet every day of the week.

LILLY. Not even when you've just been awarded a bursary?

ERNA. Of course I'm happy. Listen, Lilly – why don't you pop back up to the studio, just in case the Wooden Artefact turns up. He promised to help out getting things ready – (*To* LOUISE.) We're going to have a bit of a party, God help us. That's why we came down – we want to invite you to grace it with your presence.

LOUISE. That's very kind – but I'm not sure I'll be able to . . .

ERNA (*to* LILLY). Go on – hurry up. If there's no one there when he arrives, he'll have a temper tantrum and storm off.

LILLY. Don't be long, will you?

ERNA. No, I won't.

LILLY. It's just – it's a bit unnerving being on your own with a man who just sits and stares into space.

LILLY *leaves.* ERNA *walks up to* LOUISE *and fixes her with her stare.*

ERNA. You're not going to get yourself ill again, are you?

LOUISE. Why do you say that?

ERNA. You look shattered. You're as white as a ghost and – what is the matter?

I know you've been crying, don't pretend you haven't. You're talking to an expert in the field. It's not by any means the first time I've seen it.

LOUISE. I just had a bad night.

ERNA. Oh, I see. That's all, is it?

And – by the way – how often exactly does Alland come to call?

LOUISE. Not often. Every now and then. Recently, not very much at all, as it happens. But then, I'm not at home myself very much . . .

ERNA. You're not very practised at this game, are you?

LOUISE. What do you mean?

ERNA. Lying. I don't think you should stay here much longer.

LOUISE. Thanks for your advice, but –

ERNA. You've lost so much weight! I know all the signs!

LOUISE. But, Erna –

ERNA. I know I shouldn't say this – but I will anyway. Be careful of Alland. He's a brute.

LOUISE. What do you know about him?

ERNA. I know him through a friend of mine. He made her life hell – and then he dumped her.

LOUISE. That's not true! They agreed to part. They both got tired of each other.

ERNA. *What?*

LOUISE. He told me all about it.

ERNA. He did, did he? (*She regains her composure.*) Well, yes. It's true. That's part of his plan of attack. And he mentions no names, of course. But he touches up the picture – remember that, he touches it up – flatteringly, particularly with regards to himself.

LOUISE. But why on earth do you think that I –

ERNA. Because I just met him. Outside.

LOUISE (*happily*). Here? Outside?

ERNA. Yes, yes. He looked as if he was on his way here, but when he saw me he dodged around the corner.

LOUISE. He drops in sometimes, when he happens to be passing.

ERNA. Well. Are you going to come tonight?

LOUISE. Where?

ERNA. Have you forgotten already? Only five minutes ago I rather condescendingly issued an invitation.

LOUISE (*laughs*). Yes – of course I remember. But I'm not sure . . . perhaps I'll pop in for a little while.

ERNA. I see. You're too kind. (*She fixes* LOUISE *with a beady eye*.) Are you expecting Alland, then?

LOUISE. He hasn't been for such a long time, you see, and –

ERNA. Not for at least two days, I'd say. That is such a long time, isn't it?

LOUISE. Erna, please don't get annoyed, but do you mind if I ask you to leave now?

ERNA. Oh, for God's sake!

ERNA *leaves*.

LOUISE *paces anxiously. She fiddles with her hair, tries to distract herself with a book, but cannot settle*.

ALLAND *enters. He walks up to* LOUISE, *kisses her on the forehead*.

LOUISE. At last! I was beginning to think I would never see you again.

ALLAND (*dryly*). We don't want to get ourselves stuck in a rut, do we?

LOUISE. Were you angry with me?

ALLAND. No – but I come here to see you. Not all your friends!

LOUISE. I'm not seeing them any more.

ALLAND. The last time I came, they were all in here. So it would hardly have made any difference if I was present or not.

LOUISE (*abject*). Please come – as often as you used to.

ALLAND. I don't want to have to share you.

LOUISE (*on the brink of tears*). I've been miserable these last few days.

ALLAND. Never mind. I'm here now. And – what's this? A new dress. For my benefit?

LOUISE. No! (*She laughs*.) Yes. It is.

ALLAND. There's a new light in your eyes, lately. And you've learned to laugh.

LOUISE *lowers her eyes from his scrutiny.*

Still black, though, your dress. Still always black. Well – it's beautiful in spite of that. But it needs flowers!

He takes some roses from the vase and attaches them to her shoulder.

There – that's better already.

Look at you – so thin and fragile. If you were swathed in gauze and silk and lace, you'd be like an unearthly creature, a spirit child from a story. Do you realise how young you look? And how radiant?

LOUISE. The world has never looked as beautiful to me as it looks now. I'm seeing it all with new eyes – the sun, the flowers, this big, old, beautiful city with its grey bridges and its street lamps all reflected in the river. It takes my breath away.

ALLAND. You've become almost beautiful yourself.

LOUISE. I wish I was. I know you admire beautiful people, don't you?

ALLAND. I'd admire you, even if you weren't.

LOUISE (*putting her hand in his*). Thank you. That means more to me than if you had said I was beautiful.

ALLAND. You're a funny one, aren't you? When I first saw you, you were like some poor, straggly, wounded little bird. (*He leads her to a mirror.*) Are you really that same woman?

LOUISE. All my friends say I've grown quite young.

ALLAND. Sit here and let me be your chambermaid.

She sits – he loosens her hair.

Where's your comb? What beautiful, thick hair you've got. Now, look how gently and gracefully it falls onto your forehead. This is the same stuff you insist on torturing by pinning it back so brutally. This is how you ought to treat it – and like this –

And like this! Well? What do you think?

LOUISE. I like it.

ALLAND. So will you spare me that horrible bun in future?

LOUISE. Yes.

ALLAND. This is how I like you.

He kisses her.

LOUISE. Then I'm happy.

ALLAND. Then put your arms around me! Of your own volition. Show me how much you've grown since we've become friends. Show me that now you're free and strong and will follow your true spirit.

LOUISE *gets up hesitantly. He smiles into her face.*

Look at you, my Lulu.

Can I call you that?

LOUISE. Of course. But it still scares me.

ALLAND (*embracing her*). You're passionate, my Lulu, but are you strong?

LOUISE. Do I need to be strong? I have you, haven't I?

ALLAND. But what about when you haven't got me any longer?

LOUISE. What do you mean?

ALLAND. I've told you – love doesn't last for ever.

LOUISE *retreats.*

You too will hate me one day.

LOUISE. No. I won't.

ALLAND (*gently*). How do you know? If you were shipwrecked, on a raft in the middle of the ocean with no one but me, and if one of us had to die – you'd go at me with tooth and claw. That's human nature – you, me, all of us.

LOUISE. Don't talk like that. Please.

ALLAND. Show me a love that just rolls over quietly, and dies.

LOUISE. I'd rather die than hurt you.

ALLAND. You can't say that. Not until you're standing there, all alone.

LOUISE. Alone? After –

ALLAND. After all this happiness.

LOUISE. You're scaring me.

ALLAND. I want you to come to me without any illusions.

LOUISE. I don't understand you! Just now, I thought –

But now I don't know what to think!

ALLAND. Look at me.

He leans close to her and makes her look at him.

What can you see?

LOUISE *is embarrassed.*

You can see the truth in my eyes. But I never shackle myself to anyone. And I don't shackle anyone else to me, either. That's what I want you to understand.

LOUISE. But that's –

ALLAND. That's freedom! That's joy, and life – for you, who has never truly lived it before.

LOUISE. That's a life I don't want to live.

ALLAND. You mean you're too scared to. So be it. Follow your nature.

LOUISE (*pleading*). Don't get angry.

ALLAND. When you're being such a coward?

LOUISE. It's not cowardice.

ALLAND. So what is it? Do I disgust you?

LOUISE. No – but to talk of love only as a temporary thing, a loan –

ALLAND. I never speak of love. When it's there, it shines out of my eyes, it emanates from my entire being. What do you want? Assurances, promises, vows . . . That I'll 'love you for ever', that I'll –

LOUISE. No. I don't even ask for that. The desire – the honest intention – would be enough.

ALLAND. I have every intention of living and of clinging on to life – but that doesn't mean I'll be able to add so much as a second to my allotted time span. It's exactly the same with love.

LOUISE. You haven't understood what I'm saying.

ALLAND. Women always say that.

LOUISE. Let's change the subject, shall we? Let's just go back to how it was before.

ALLAND. How it was before! It can never, ever be the way it was before. It might be more, or it might be less than it was before. But it could never be the same. So it's your choice.

LOUISE. I couldn't survive without your friendship.

ALLAND. What delusions! Women can turn anything into a lie.

He picks up his hat to leave.

LOUISE. Please stay!

ALLAND. Don't look so tragic! I'll stay if Mademoiselle so wishes.

But it's going to be awkward for both of us.

He sits. A silence.

It's not me you're fighting, it's yourself. You're wrestling with your own spirit, it's down on the ground, your fingers are around its throat, it's gasping for air – but I won't move a muscle to help you.

LOUISE. Why are you like this? Gustave – please, be like you were just now.

ALLAND. What can I say? (*In formal conversation mode*.) Allow me to tell you a story. Please be seated – over there. Don't worry. I would never try to take something that was not freely offered. You could travel the world with me in perfect safety. I wouldn't lay a finger on you, I wouldn't get even a hair's breadth closer to you than I am now, Mademoiselle Strandberg.

LOUISE. Call me Lulu.

ALLAND. Why would I call you 'Lulu'? There is no intimacy between us. We are two strangers – and that's how you want it to be. Aren't you interested in my story?

LOUISE. Yes, of course I am.

ALLAND. It's about me, of course. Artists who have hit a block and men of a certain age always talk about themselves. Have you noticed that?

LOUISE. Well –

ALLAND. At the moment I'm modelling the bust of a lady. She's very attractive – really ugly women rarely commission me. I have the reputation for doing nothing to improve on their looks.

LOUISE. There are plenty of sculptors who do, I'm sure. They make their subjects appear more beautiful and then, I believe, they charge a higher fee.

ALLAND. Really?

Well, the woman I'm working on at the moment has one of those faces which is very hard to portray, because it is the expression that's so captivating, the mobility of the features, rather than the features themselves. It's not a regular, conventional beauty she has – it's something more profound, a beauty of the soul. When you speak to her, you can feel it – it's electrifying. It's that mysterious allure that certain women possess, and know they possess.

LOUISE *can't stop herself from fidgeting*.

I immediately felt sorry for her – she seems so lonely. She's married to a Hungarian tycoon who lives only for his horses, and the racetrack. He's impossibly rich, he has dozens of mistresses, and he thoroughly neglects his wife.

LOUISE. Even though she's so very beautiful?

ALLAND. His fancy seems to be taking him elsewhere. Besides, as we already know, beauty's power is transient.

LOUISE. And what about her?

ALLAND. She's noble, through and through. And proud. She's sophisticated and gorgeous. She has a gaggle of admirers, but finds them vacuous and dull. She plays with them like puppies, casts them aside and scolds them when they begin to bore her. It's not her fault – she's not a snob, but she just doesn't love any of them. And she's longing for someone to love. Because, for all its lavishness, her life is utterly empty.

LOUISE (*with an effort*). Have you known her long?

ALLAND. It feels as if we've known each other for years.

Are you all right? You look rather pale.

LOUISE. I'm fine.

ALLAND. Women like her have an extraordinary hold over me. So completely self-possessed, and clear-sighted – simultaneously free, yet aloof – virginal, almost. She's got the full weight of class and power behind her, as well as her own intellect. The refinement of generations flows in her blood. Just the way she dresses is –

Well, I can't help liking it when a woman dresses well. I know that's something you rather despise.

LOUISE (*with mounting distress*). No! I don't – I . . .

ALLAND. I feel as if her entrapment of me has already begun. I'll fall victim one of these fine days.

LOUISE *staggers*.

Whatever is the matter?

He looks into her face, smiling.

God – is it that painful to hear the truth?

He takes her hand and kisses it. LOUISE *pulls back
sharply.*

LOUISE. No! Do you really think I'm that gullible and naive?
Just because I haven't lived in the big, wide world as you
have? But you're so very wrong. I know what you're doing.
I always knew. All I wanted was – I only wanted to – to
find out how this particular Don Juan would go about it.
You've been blinded by your own self-obsession. You've
fallen into my trap –

ALLAND (*picking up his hat*). Then you can't have sprung it
very well, because now I'm off.

LOUISE. It's been fascinating for me to observe a philanderer
in action – the renowned artist, the seducer of women –

But what about you? What's your excuse?

ALLAND. There's only ever been one motive, which is not
one that I wish to dissect. If a bird is singing, what would
you rather do? Cut it open, and stuff it, and seal it in a glass
box? Or would you rather just leave it to sing freely, and
delight in its song?

LOUISE. Birds, birds, birds! Why do you always talk about
birds!

Well, all right then, what kind of a prize would a drab old
pigeon like me have been for you? Why do you keep luring
me in? What do you *want* from me?

ALLAND (*coolly*). I don't want anything. I'm drifting along to
see where the river of life takes me.

I came to you as one human being to another – open,
trusting and without ulterior motives. I just liked you!

Then I got to know you, and I liked you even more.

So then I wanted to touch your hand, and kiss you, and hold you.

Is that so outrageous? It's such a natural thing – it's like breathing: I like you – I want you – I hold you.

And you put your arms around me, and returned my affection.

So I thought.

When all along, all you really wanted was to gain some sexual experience. You, with your strict moral principles! Shame on you, you naughty woman!

LOUISE *sits, covers her face, cries.* ALLAND *paces nervously.*

Look – I'm sorry. I am. But what can I do? This is all so unpleasant.

And what a vain idiot I was, to give you my bust. I'm sure you'll be glad to get that out of your way.

LOUISE. No – not that too! Can't I at least keep the portrait?

ALLAND (*moved by her despair*). Don't take it so hard.

LOUISE. Please, can I just keep your portrait?

ALLAND. Yes. Of course, if you want it.

If only you could just have let it evolve, this thing between us. Why did you have to ruin it by poking at it with your great, big stick?

LOUISE. Yes, I know. Why? God! – Why?

ALLAND. Did you think I didn't care, just because of that story I told you?

LOUISE. Yes!

ALLAND. And then I suppose you felt ashamed that you hadn't rebuffed me earlier?

LOUISE. Yes.

ALLAND. You can't expect to understand someone like me.

Don't even try. I can't measure up to your bourgeois little yardstick. It just won't work. I don't recognise the same standards.

'Why?' you ask. 'Why?' The question is unworthy of you. What does a question like that mean? How can I explain why I want to kiss a woman? If I didn't feel it, I wouldn't do it!

LOUISE. It was so painful for me to hear you. I can't understand it myself –

ALLAND. You were afraid that I'd think you were too 'easy'.

LOUISE. Yes.

ALLAND (*suddenly tender*). How could you be that – with those eyes of yours, and that forehead, and that mouth?

LOUISE. If you knew where I come from, how I was brought up – you might understand, and forgive me.

ALLAND. You poor creature! You've had a tough life. It's made you all suspicious and defensive. You acted out of self-defence. You thought you were going to be hurt, and you instinctively lashed out. I should have understood that at the time.

LOUISE. Yes. I think I was afraid that you'd touched me too deeply.

ALLAND (*smiling*). And you don't think that now?

LOUISE *smiles back*.

(*Joking*.) Then, with your permission, I should perhaps withdraw?

LOUISE. Stay a bit longer.

ALLAND. Actually, I can't. (*He checks his pocket watch*.) I've already kept Her Ladyship waiting for over an hour. I won't get much work done today.

LOUISE. But . . . please –

ALLAND. Please don't ask me to be rude to a lady!

LOUISE. So I shan't see you again today?

ALLAND. I can't make any promises.

LOUISE. Please, try and come back!

ALLAND *bows, kisses her hand.*

ALLAND. *Au revoir. A bientot, peut-être!*

He leaves.

LOUISE *watches through the window as he leaves. She examines the part of her hand that he kissed, then presses her lips against it.*

Outside, voices can be heard.

CONCIERGE. I'm telling you – she's not at home.

ERNA. Stop arguing, you silly old trout!

ERNA *enters, with the* CONCIERGE *hot on her heels.*

CONCIERGE. She just barged her way in, ignoring everything I've said –

ERNA. I need to talk to Mademoiselle Strandberg.

CONCIERGE. I've been trying to tell her that you're not at home!

ERNA. But there she is – right in front of us.

CONCIERGE. So she is.

LOUISE (*to the* CONCIERGE). Would you leave us alone, please.

CONCIERGE. Fine. Fine! I'll let the whole of Paris in then, next time.

CONCIERGE *exits.*

ERNA (*agitated*). I need to talk to you.

LOUISE. Well, sit yourself down then, Erna.

ERNA. Thanks. (*She stands in front of* LOUISE.) I'll get straight to the point. It's about Alland.

LOUISE. Alland?

ERNA. I know he's just left. I've been waiting until he did.

LOUISE looks at her.

You said that he'd told you this story about a woman, a painter, who –

LOUISE. Yes, yes –

ERNA. That was me.

A beat.

LOUISE. I know all about it. Everything.

ERNA. No you don't. All you know is what he's told you. That's very different from how it really was.

LOUISE. He wouldn't lie.

ERNA. No, but he paints it in different colours! He mesmerises you to see it all through his eyes and – (*Forcing herself to be calm.*) He told you that they both tired of each other?

LOUISE. Yes.

ERNA. He did. Not me. But I left him. I told him that it was over, for me as well.

LOUISE. Then it's not his fault! It's your fault.

ERNA. I have some pride. I won't settle for pity from a man who was once in love with me.

LOUISE. But didn't you know, from the outset, that that's how it would end?

ERNA. It doesn't make any difference what you know! Little by little, he draws you in, he preaches to you about free love, he feeds you little scraps of real emotion, and then – in spite of all your best intentions – you succumb to your own illusions.

LOUISE casts down her eyes. ERNA takes her hand.

I think you should leave Paris, Louise.

LOUISE. I can't.

No – don't worry. Nothing's happened between us.

ERNA. I know how often he comes to see you. If it's not today, it'll be tomorrow . . . or the next day. He's a bloodsucker. He won't let go unless you force him to. Tear him out before he's gnawed his way right into your flesh.

Leave Paris.

LOUISE. It's not what you think. I'm strong enough to keep him at a safe distance.

ERNA. You're even weaker than I was –

LOUISE. I daren't leave. I need to see him, and hear him talk, and if I'm deprived of that the desire becomes so strong –

ERNA. You think it's safer to stay?

LOUISE. Yes.

ERNA. You're an innocent. You don't know what you're doing.

LOUISE (*meeting her gaze*). I do. I do know what I'm doing.

ERNA. Just because you've resisted the temptation a couple of times, do you think that makes you strong? It'll come again. And in the end, he'll get you. He'll use any means at his disposal. He'll torture you.

She imitates ALLAND *at his most seductive.*

'Only if you come to me of your own free will . . . Be brave!' And then: 'Why it is that work always makes me long for happiness, for love – I become quite defenceless.' And then: 'She's so wealthy and gorgeous – completely free-thinking, but cultured, and well-bred. I don't know why women like her have so much power over me – no doubt I'll become her victim.'

LOUISE *turns away.*

What he's really good at, is putting the knife in an open wound and twisting. You think it'll kill you, the agony of it. But then you start to believe you can catch him – even though he himself assures you that you can't.

But you'll never catch him. He's a slippery eel. You might
make a little mark on him – draw a little blood, perhaps.
But you'll never catch him and keep him.

LOUISE. Did he tell you all that – about the lady that he's
sculpting?

ERNA (*nods*). That little tale is etched on my memory. That's
what tipped me over the edge. It was after that that I fell.

LOUISE. Do you think it was true?

ERNA. There will always be some little princess who's sitting
for him. And he knows how to use her to his advantage. He
turns her into a lure in his hunt for women. I realised that,
afterwards. I went over it, step by step. It's easy to be wise
with hindsight. And then I was so furious to have been
taken in – I wanted to tear out my hair with my own hands.

But there was nothing I could have done at the time. The
thought of him lavishing that adoration – which should
have been for me – on someone else . . . I couldn't stand it.
I knew I had to choose: give myself to him, or give him up
altogether.

I couldn't give him up.

So. That's what happened.

LOUISE. And were you happy, then?

ERNA. Oh yes. It was incredible.

No. No, actually, that's not true. I'm forgetting the misery!
The humiliation. The waiting! He could be loving.
Sometimes. And sometimes he wasn't.

He's always after someone. He is so small. For all his
greatness – so small, so vain. And when it comes to women,
he's a liability.

LOUISE. God – look at you! You can't look like that when
you speak about it, and pretend you haven't known the most
tremendous happiness.

ERNA. I've known all the torments of hell! You don't know
what it's like to have that, and then lose it.

LOUISE. But at least you have the memory of it. A memory
like that must illuminate the rest of your life.

ERNA. Illuminated by a memory! No. Just the opposite, in
fact. He's been in fifty, sixty – a hundred pairs of female
arms before he came to ours. And every one of them was
told, in that delicious voice, 'You're a good person. I feel
such admiration for you.'

LOUISE. But do you think that voice always sounds so true?

ERNA. Oh yes. That's why it's so dangerous. He exists only
in the moment. He gives each of us a tiny part of himself,
a little dollop of real feeling. That's why there's so little left.
He's been spreading himself very thinly.

LOUISE. Yes. I might have allowed things to go too far. I've
been weak. I should have told him to –

But what if he's *right*? Surely I must make a choice. It's not
tenable any more.

ERNA. Will you leave, then?

LOUISE. I've got to get away. I've never been really tempted
before, not like this.

ERNA. And until you go, tell me you'll close your door to him.

LOUISE. Yes.

Only – not tonight. I can't leave without saying goodbye.
I couldn't bear it.

But tomorrow –

ERNA. You'll leave.

LOUISE. I think so.

ERNA. You don't know what you think any more!

LOUISE. I can't leave without telling him what he's meant
to me.

ERNA. Dangerous tactics.

LOUISE. Sometimes I do think that –

Well, that he loves me.

ERNA. That's what I thought.

LOUISE. But what if he asked me to marry him?

ERNA. God! That's what we all think! But he'd never allow
his emotions to outwit his intellect. He'd never let himself
be shackled. 'Love is transient,' as he says. And then when
it's all over, he'll plant a kiss on your hand, and off he'll go.

And there you are.

All on your own.

LOUISE *shudders*.

Go home. Cut your losses. You're not as strong as I was,
and I really suffered.

I was so abject, I revered him. There I was, scrabbling
about in the dust at his feet. But now, it's all over. The pain
has toughened me up. Look at me now! I'm his equal. My
work hangs side by side with his. Hatred bred strength, and
the desire to succeed. If you can hate, you can survive.

LOUISE. I don't think I can.

ERNA. That's why you've got to go. Go and bury yourself in
lovely, homely things, and try to block out the memory.

LOUISE. Yes, I do want to get back home. I feel as if I've
been locked up in an underground, troll world, where the
only light is fire, and the only pleasure is torturing humans.

Maybe it'll save me, if I can just get back to the sunshine,
and those green woods, and the cold wind from the sea.

ALLAND *enters. Seeing* ERNA, *he bows coldly. Then he
walks up to* LOUISE *and kisses her hand*.

ALLAND. I wasn't needed, after all. So here I am.

LOUISE. Thank you. I didn't expect –

She glances at ERNA.

ALLAND. I'm not sure if Mademoiselle Wallden remembers
me – if she does, she always fails to acknowledge me –

ERNA *leaves with an air of defiance*.

(*A little flustered*.) Now there's a woman who knows how to maintain her dignity.

But what's up with you?

LOUISE. Nothing. I'm fine.

ALLAND (*taking her hand*). Tell me – has Mademoiselle Wallden . . . ? Look at me, at least! Or is it something I've done? Have I hurt you in some way?

LOUISE. And if you had – would it matter?

ALLAND. Would it matter if I'd hurt you? What do you mean!

LOUISE. Nothing. Nothing. I'm just feeling a bit emotional.

ALLAND. Why?

LOUISE. I'm just like that. You'd think I was silly.

ALLAND. No, now I do want to know.

LOUISE. I'm leaving Paris.

ALLAND. When?

LOUISE. Tomorrow.

ALLAND. Have you had some news from home?

LOUISE. No.

ALLAND. So why . . . Is it because of me?

LOUISE. Yes.

ALLAND. Am I that dangerous?

You funny creature! Not quite a girl, not quite a woman.

LOUISE. I'm a woman who is old enough to understand the mistakes I'm making.

ALLAND. Don't be coy. You know you're young! You look young, you feel young, but you don't have the emotions of a woman.

LOUISE *remains silent*.

Isn't that true?

LOUISE. No.

ALLAND. You're incapable of love.

LOUISE. I mustn't. I won't.

ALLAND. Do you really think that love takes any notice of 'mustn't' and 'won't'?

LOUISE. No – unfortunately.

He pulls her to him.

No!

She puts her arms around his neck, rests her head on his chest.

ALLAND. Lulu, your whole body is crying out, 'Yes!' Every nerve, every sinew –

LOUISE. No. I'm sorry. It's against everything I believe in.

ALLAND. What do women understand about what they want! In that way, at least, you are a real woman.

He releases her.

Go on then, Lulu. Go. Your Nordic soul doesn't understand much about passion.

LOUISE. Don't be harsh. This is painful for me! We are going to be parted – or do you want me to stay? I'd do anything – except that.

ALLAND. It's everything, or nothing. If you choose nothing, you might as well go.

LOUISE. I've known such exultation. I've felt a kind of wild joy, as if thousands of birds have been set free, and are wheeling around my head.

When I'm with you, misery and unhappiness seem like far away things – too remote to even remember.

But when you aren't with me, it feels as if the world is drained of happiness. You can see what happens to me on the days when I don't see you.

I think I'll go mad, or die.

There's no point talking about 'friendship' or 'affection'.
I love you, utterly and irredeemably.

ALLAND. Is there no redemption in love?

LOUISE. I don't think so.

ALLAND. Time heals all things.

LOUISE. Not this.

ALLAND (*amicably*). You poor thing! I don't understand you –
you're so different from me – but I do feel sorry for you.
It's authentic, your unhappiness. I'd like to help you, if I
can. I'll try to be unselfish. You had better leave. You're not
tough enough for the life here. You'd be better off back
home. Find yourself a nice husband, live in peace and quiet,
according to your nature and your principles.

LOUISE. I can't.

ALLAND. Be strong. Go.

LOUISE. You're so good. That's what makes it hard.

ALLAND. Me, good! No one's ever said that before.

LOUISE. Not even someone who loved you?

ALLAND. No one.

LOUISE. I know you are good. You deserve to be happy.

ALLAND. Life doesn't always dish out what we deserve.

LOUISE. You know me so little. I've been so in awe of you
that I haven't been able to talk to you properly.

ALLAND. I know you've seen my faults clearly enough. I've
never hidden them from you.

LOUISE. That's why I saw what's good in you. What's great.

ALLAND. Have you?

So you don't think it's true what people say – that I'm
finished, as an artist?

LOUISE. No.

ALLAND (*energetically*). No! And I'm going to show them you're right.

LOUISE (*taking his hands*). Please do. Please do!

ALLAND. Do you really care whether I'm successful or not?

LOUISE. How little you know me!

ALLAND (*slowly, looking into her face*). Yes. There's so much going on in this head of yours. More than I realised.

He takes her head in his hands and kisses her forehead.

Adieu, Lulu. Thank you. Think of me, from time to time.

LOUISE. I will. Always.

ALLAND (*looking into her eyes*). Could I really be happy? Could I be calm and contented, like other people? Sometimes I think I could. It's not much, what I ask – but she'd have to be infinitely gentle, the woman I could spend my life with, because I'm so restless and neurotic . . . I haven't met many women like that in my life.

LOUISE. How many?

ALLAND. Two.

LOUISE. That's one too many.

ALLAND *kisses her hand, and leaves.* LOUISE *sinks to the floor.*

ACT THREE

A rainy July day in a small, provincial town in Sweden. A sitting room with old-fashioned, stiffly arranged furniture. White dust sheets cover the sofa and chairs. There's a table covered with a clean white cloth; white curtains at the window. Hand-woven runners form a cross on the floor. There are flowers – fuchsia, geraniums and cacti – on the windowsill. In the hall, visible through a door, the brick floor is covered with juniper branches in the traditional way. Other doors lead to the kitchen and the dining room. LOUISE, dressed in a cotton frock, is sitting at the window staring out. BOTILDA enters with coffee cups on a tray and places them with elaborate care on the table.

LOUISE. Does it always rain like this?

BOTILDA. You know it does, pet. It always rains when the hay's just been cut.

LOUISE. Not one single day of sunshine since I got back. Not a single day when it's looked any better out there than it does today.

BOTILDA. How do you want it to look? That is what it looks like. That's what it always looks like.

LOUISE. Yes. That's what I mean.

BOTILDA. If you ask my opinion – not that it's any of my business – but if going abroad just makes a person miserable when they get back, whatever is the point of going in the first place?

LOUISE. That's very true, Botilda. It's always best to just stay put. (*She gets up.*) What day is it today?

BOTILDA. What a question! You know very well it's your birthday.

LOUISE. I know. But what day of the week is it?

BOTILDA. It's Wednesday, of course – market day.

LOUISE. I can't believe it – is it really only two weeks since I arrived home? It was a Wednesday, wasn't it?

BOTILDA. Yes.

LOUISE. Fourteen days ago. It feels like fourteen years. It feels as if life itself has just fallen asleep, and there it sits, motionless, slumbering – getting slowly covered over with dust.

BOTILDA. Lordy me, I'm sure we can keep on top of the dust!

LOUISE *sits down and bursts into tears at the table*.

Look out, pet – what are you doing? That's a clean cloth!

BOTILDA *flusters around, straightening the tablecloth.* LOUISE *gets up but can't stop crying*.

I don't know what's got into you since you got back from that wretched Paris. You're just not yourself any more.

LOUISE. No.

BOTILDA. You're not going the same way as Agnes, are you?

LOUISE. Oh God, don't say that. I'd slit my wrists.

BOTILDA. Don't say such a thing! We stay here on this earth for as long as the Good Lord wants us to stay.

LOUISE *goes back to staring out of the window*.

Oh my word, what are we going to do with you? We can't have you crying on your birthday. That's not a good sign. Not good at all.

LOUISE. I can't help it!

BOTILDA. What have you got to worry about? You're a very popular girl. Just you wait till I tell you what I saw this morning on the way to the market.

LOUISE. Don't.

BOTILDA. Six o'clock in the morning, and there he was, out and about – the bank manager is who I'm talking about, of course – and you'll never guess what he was doing.

LOUISE. No.

BOTILDA. Picking flowers! A really nice bunch. And it's no secret who that's for!

LOUISE. He's always been very sweet, the bank manager.

BOTILDA. That's men for you! He's got his reasons.

A train whistle is heard.

LOUISE. There's the train.

BOTILDA. There'll be lots of cattle, I'm sure. It's a big cattle market – bigger than ever. Squire Svensson's bringing all three of his calves –

She goes to the window.

Yes – look at them all flooding out. Squire What's-his-name, and the Vicar of Vallby. Oh look! There's Inspector Knutson! And who's that young chappie walking next to him?

LOUISE gets up happily.

LOUISE. Viggo! It's Viggo!

She waves through the window.

BOTILDA. Well I never, it's Mr Viggo! I almost didn't recognise him. And he seems in a hurry – I'd better get a move on, he'll need a nice hot cup of coffee.

She exits to the kitchen.

LOUISE opens the door. VIGGO enters the hall.

LOUISE. Viggo! You came!

VIGGO. Happy birthday!

He takes off his travelling coat and galoshes.

There, that's better. Now, let's have a good look at you.

You look so different!

LOUISE. Do you think so?

VIGGO. What is it? Paris – or losing Mother that's done this to you?

LOUISE. Done what?

VIGGO. You've bloomed! You look beautiful.

LOUISE. Come and sit down. You must be tired after the journey.

VIGGO. Not a bit. It would take more than that to tire me out.

LOUISE. You need your rest, like everyone else.

VIGGO. Not yet, though. I'm catching the one o'clock train.

LOUISE. You're leaving! Where are you going?

VIGGO (*cheerfully*). To Paris. I got some money for my book, and I've been commissioned to do some articles for a newspaper. I'm hoping I'll be able to make ends meet.

LOUISE (*downcast*). I thought you'd be staying –

Her eyes start to well up.

VIGGO strokes her hair.

VIGGO. Cheer up – don't be sad!

BOTILDA enters with coffee.

Good morning, Botilda.

BOTILDA. Thank you, thank you. A good morning to you, too. What a nice surprise – and on her birthday, too. You're very welcome. What about a nice cup of coffee? That'll set you right after your long journey.

VIGGO. Thank you – how nice. How is everything, Botilda?

BOTILDA. Thank you, sir, everything's just fine and dandy with me. You won't hear any complaints from this old bag of bones. But Miss Louise – now that's another matter. I'm sorry, miss, but I'm telling him the way it is. And that's why it's a good thing that you're here, Mr Viggo, because if you can't cheer her up, no one can!

LOUISE. I'm afraid we won't be able to keep him here with us for long, Botilda. He's leaving on the one o'clock train.

BOTILDA. One o'clock! No! What's the hurry?

VIGGO. Nothing. (*He laughs.*) It's just that I'm going back to Paris.

BOTILDA. Back *there* again?

VIGGO *nods.*

Well, really. Can you please tell me what's so very special about that city?

VIGGO. What's so very special is the way it always makes you want to go back to it!

LOUISE. That's just the way it is.

BOTILDA. Then I'm sure it's better not to go there in the first place. Now, how about some more coffee?

VIGGO. No – thank you.

BOTILDA. I'll take it out, then. I can keep it hot out there – I thought they'd be here by now.

VIGGO. Who?

BOTILDA. What do you mean, 'who'? It's somebody's birthday, isn't it? So there will be visitors. Not that she looks very happy about the fact.

She exits.

VIGGO *takes* LOUISE*'s hand.*

VIGGO. What is it? Tell me.

LOUISE. It's nothing, Viggo. Nothing at all.

VIGGO. But I'm your confidant! You've got to tell me.

LOUISE. Oh God, I think they're coming . . .

There's a kerfuffle in the hall. Through the door we can see MRS *and* MISS KNUTSON *removing their galoshes.*

MRS KNUTSON. We don't want to bring the Flood in with us, do we now? Put the umbrellas in the corner, Agneta –

and lend me your hanky, I need to dab off the paper around the flowers, it's sopping wet . . .

LOUISE *rises to greet her guests.* MRS *and* MISS KNUTSON *enter with flowers.*

Good morning, dear Louise. Many happy returns. (*She hands over the flowers.*) Isn't this weather we're having simply frightful?

LOUISE. Thank you so much. Thank you.

MRS KNUTSON. And how nice to see that you're here, too, Mr Pihl. They told us in the shop that you'd come. To celebrate the special day, no doubt!

MISS KNUTSON *extends her hand, too.*

LOUISE. Please, come in and sit down Mrs K.

She goes to the kitchen door to give some instructions to BOTILDA.

MRS KNUTSON *takes a seat on the sofa.* MISS KNUTSON *sits at the table.*

MRS KNUTSON. Well now, how jolly. Mr Pihl, tell us some news of the big, wide world out there.

VIGGO. There's nothing much that I know of, I'm afraid. Except this awful weather!

MRS KNUTSON. We were planning an outing in the woods for last Saturday, but we couldn't possibly go in this weather. We had to call it off.

VIGGO. I can imagine.

BOTILDA *enters with coffee.*

MRS KNUTSON. Good morning, Botilda.

MISS KNUTSON. Good morning, Botilda.

LOUISE. Would you like some coffee?

MRS KNUTSON. Thank you, my dear. Yes please.

LOUISE *pours.*

We hardly recognise you, Mr Pihl! It's been such a long time – as I'm sure has been noted in my daughter's secret diary.

MISS KNUTSON *blushes and nudges her mother.*

Oh really, everyone in this town knows perfectly well what the main topic of that diary is.

MISS KNUTSON. Mother!

MRS KNUTSON. Don't worry, I won't say another word. Though you should know, Mr Pihl, that there is no shortage of marriage proposals as far as my daughter is concerned. No shortage at all!

MISS KNUTSON (*desperate to change the subject*). And how long will you be staying, Mr Pihl?

VIGGO. Until one o'clock.

MRS KNUTSON. Good gracious! We'd heard you were staying for a month. That's very disappointing, because Agneta and her friends are planning to put on a little play, and they had a part lined up for you.

VIGGO. I'm sure it'll be quite easy to find someone to replace me.

MRS KNUTSON. Easy to replace you! I hardly think so.

MISS KNUTSON. You were going to take the part of –

VIGGO. – the leading man?

MRS KNUTSON. Quite right. And the leading lady would be –

VIGGO. – Miss Strandberg, perhaps?

MRS KNUTSON. Oh no! Agneta would take the lead, of course.

VIGGO. Ah. I should have guessed.

MISS KNUTSON *giggles.*

MRS KNUTSON. Oh dear, Louise doesn't look as if she's enjoying her birthday very much.

LOUISE. Don't I?

MRS KNUTSON. I'm afraid not. Come on, Mr Pihl. Can't you do something to buck up your stepsister? She seems quite melancholic.

VIGGO. Louise is never exactly jolly.

MRS KNUTSON. But look at her, she's not herself at all this morning.

MISS KNUTSON. We're doing our best, making such a fuss of her – but we don't seem to be making any difference.

LOUISE. I'm very grateful for all your kindness . . .

MRS KNUTSON. You wouldn't have to look very far for kindness! I'm sure I know of someone who would like nothing better than to heap kindness upon you from morning till night.

BOTILDA *enters with flowers*.

BOTILDA. Mr Moller's messenger boy brought you these. I'm afraid Mr Moller won't be able to come himself until closing time at the bank. There are so many customers today, you see.

LOUISE. Thank you, Botilda.

MRS *and* MISS KNUTSON *exchange meaningful glances*.

MRS KNUTSON. Poor Mr Moller!

MISS KNUTSON *giggles*.

LOUISE. Why 'poor'?

MRS KNUTSON. He'll be stuck there at the bank all morning.

LOUISE. Would you like some more coffee, Mrs K?

MRS KNUTSON. No thank you, my dear. We wouldn't want to run you out of coffee before Mr Moller comes, would we? He's very fond of coffee – and all the more so when it's this little hand that's pouring it!

She pats LOUISE's *hand*.

LOUISE. Would anyone else like another cup?

MISS KNUTSON. Yes, please – well, just a little drop.

LOUISE. Thank you.

MRS KNUTSON. We'd better be going soon. If lunch isn't on the table at twelve o'clock, that husband of mine turns into a troll. Ah well, that's married life for you!

MISS KNUTSON. But Mother –

MRS KNUTSON. Of course, you're right, darling. It's a wonderful thing, really, marriage.

She extends her hand to say goodbye.

How old are you today, my dear, if you don't mind my asking?

LOUISE. Thirty-two.

MRS KNUTSON. Gracious! (*Laughing.*) Then it's high time. Goodbye, my regards to Mr Moller!

MISS KNUTSON. Goodbye. Happy birthday. Give my regards, too. (*She giggles.*)

MRS KNUTSON. Goodbye, Mr Pihl. 'Bon voyage!'

VIGGO. Thank you very much.

When they've gone, LOUISE *returns and closes the door behind her.*

Phew!

LOUISE *goes back to the window.*

BOTILDA *re-enters with a tray and starts to clear away the cups.*

BOTILDA. Lordy, what a lot of flowers! I've never seen so many in my life. And all Madam can do is to sit there like a wet weekend.

She exits to the kitchen.

VIGGO. What is it, Lou? You can tell *me*, surely.

LOUISE. I don't really know myself. I feel strange – a stranger, in my own home. And I'm *always* cold.

VIGGO. You're missing Paris.

LOUISE. Yes.

VIGGO. I can imagine how it is here for you. Loneliness stares out at you from every corner. This was your family home, where you grew up, with all the people you loved – but now there's only you left.

LOUISE. It's more than that. People are very kind, of course, but I don't really feel I belong here any more. They fill their days with things which are so irrelevant to me. The things that interest them are so tiny, so trivial. Yet their insinuations are hobnailed.

VIGGO. You mean . . .

LOUISE. I mean all the giggling, the significant looks, the heavy hints. It's hideous.

VIGGO. Isn't there anyone here who you can be friends with?

LOUISE (*shaking her head*). In these last two weeks my hair's gone grey and I feel as though my heart has just frozen solid.

VIGGO. Louise!

LOUISE. Do you remember that old story about a young girl who becomes the bride of the King of the Mountain Trolls? There's something about a spell – the splendour of the troll world casts a spell on her and, once she's seen it, she's always longing to get back to it. That's how I feel. I've been bewitched by a world which isn't mine.

VIGGO. Me too.

LOUISE. You're all right, though – you can go back there, and gather up your bride . . . but I –

What am I?

Nothing! I'm in love with a shadow. I can't have him, so what we have is just a fantasy, it's not real.

VIGGO. Why can't you have him?

LOUISE. Because I believe that love should be wholehearted, for ever. But he . . .

It's against everything I believe in, Viggo. It's against my nature to give your love just temporarily. Just for a bit.

VIGGO (*moved*). When love starts to germinate, when its roots go down and its leaves come up, it's not right that it shouldn't be allowed to flower. It must feel that if you cut off the bud, the whole plant will wither. Is that how it feels? That its roots are so deep inside you that if it dies, you die with it?

LOUISE. Yes, Viggo. That's exactly it.

VIGGO. It's hard for you, Lou.

LOUISE. I can't recognise my old self any more, in these quiet little low-ceilinged rooms, with the dust sheets shrouding everything. Was that little girl me? Did I play in here? Did I believe in God, and feel strong and confident in all my beliefs?

VIGGO. You've got to take care of yourself, and your future.

LOUISE. What future? When I think about living here, in this cold place for ever –

When I think about the years coming and going, and never seeing him, not even hearing his voice –

Day after day, and not even a letter – then all those days and weeks and years don't seem bearable. Where would be the joy, or the beauty? Just empty rooms.

So I wrote to him.

I'm not sure quite what I said. I was just trying not to be forgotten.

VIGGO. How long ago was that?

LOUISE. I'm not sure. I don't know what's happened to the days, they don't seem to end any more. Time's lost all its shape – but the emptiness hasn't. I know all the different shapes of the emptiness.

VIGGO. And if he does ask you to come to him?

LOUISE. I'll go! Blindly. Immediately. I won't think twice about the consequences.

VIGGO (*stroking her forehead*). I won't make it worse for you by giving you any advice. Maybe you'll see it differently when you've calmed down a bit.

From the hall there is the sound of galoshes being removed and an umbrella falling on the floor. There is a knock at the door, and MR MOLLER, *the bank manager, enters.*

MR MOLLER (*bows*). Miss Louise, I'm so sorry I wasn't able to get away sooner. But I would have been loath to deny myself the pleasure of paying my respects to you personally.

LOUISE. Thank you for the flowers. It was a very kind thought.

MR MOLLER. My pleasure! Good morning, Mr Pihl. Just a short visit, this time, I hear?

VIGGO. That's right.

MR MOLLER. I'm sure Miss Louise will be sorry to see you leave so soon.

LOUISE. Of course. But I'm glad to have seen him, even briefly.

MR MOLLER. I expect the train will be very crowded.

VIGGO (*looking at his watch*). And I'll have to sort out my luggage. I should probably be going now.

LOUISE. Already?

VIGGO (*looking her in the eyes*). Would you like me to stay?

LOUISE. Thank you, Viggo, but no. You must go.

VIGGO (*taking her hand*). Goodbye, then.

LOUISE (*tears in her eyes*). Goodbye. Say hello to Paris for me.

VIGGO. Goodbye.

He shakes hands with MR MOLLER.

MR MOLLER. Have a pleasant journey.

VIGGO. Thank you. (*He goes to the kitchen door*.) Bye,
Botilda! I'm off now!

BOTILDA (*entering, drying her hands on her apron*). Goodbye.
Oh! Mr Moller! I didn't know you were here! No one told
me! I'll get the coffee!

MR MOLLER. Not for me, thank you.

LOUISE. Perhaps I can offer you a glass of wine?

MR MOLLER. Thanks, but to be perfectly honest, it would go
to my head at this time in the morning.

VIGGO (*now in coat and galoshes, from the hall*). Goodbye!

LOUISE. Bye bye, Viggo.

BOTILDA. Mr Moller, you're most welcome to sit here and
keep Miss Louise company, or she'll get so very mopey.

BOTILDA *exits*.

MR MOLLER. I'm happy to stay for a little while, if you
don't mind, Miss Louise?

LOUISE. As if I'd mind, Mr Moller!

MR MOLLER. Tell me, honestly – are you very sad that Viggo
is leaving?

LOUISE. Yes. This place does feel very lonely.

MR MOLLER (*with compassion*). Is there anything I can do?
I mean –

The sound of train whistles comes from the station.

LOUISE. The next one will be Viggo's train.

MR MOLLER. Yes.

Silence.

LOUISE (*trying to pull herself together*). So you've finished
for the day, have you?

MR MOLLER. Oh no – luckily there's plenty of work to keep me busy all afternoon.

LOUISE. Do you like working?

MR MOLLER. It's the only thing that helps when your spirits are low.

LOUISE. I wish I could work.

MR MOLLER. Your work, Miss Louise, should be to make a home beautiful and light.

LOUISE. I want a man's work. I can see how it distracts you from unhappiness. You can get engrossed and devote yourself to it – for hour after hour. Numbers lined up in rows on paper – crowding into your head and blocking out all other thoughts –

Time must pass without you even realising. And then it's the end of the day, and you're tired both mentally and physically. And how wonderful it must be then, lying down to sleep a dreamless sleep, replenishing your strength for another day of work.

MR MOLLER. Don't talk like that! You seem so sad, Miss Louise. (*He takes her hand.*) What's happened? What's weighing you down like this? It'll help to talk about it. If you can still trust your old friend?

LOUISE. Yes, but –

MR MOLLER. Is it because of losing your mother? You're all alone here in what was your family home. Perhaps you need to get away – a change of scene might help.

LOUISE. Yes.

MR MOLLER. Do you remember that summer when I saw you for the first time? You were just a child, and you sat on my knee to do your French homework. You sat there so happily, as if that was your place, and always would be. I was your 'big friend'. You used to say you didn't like anyone better than me. And sometimes you'd fling your arms round my neck and kiss me.

It's such a long time ago now, but I remember it so well. Then you grew up, and never sat on my lap again. You seemed to forget that I was your big friend. But I've never forgotten. I've been remembering for twenty years.

And this isn't the first time that I've asked you, but it will be the last time, Louise. You may think I'm being too persistent, but you were very young the last time I asked you. I can understand why you wanted to see something of the world first.

And now that you're all alone, and you've seen – perhaps – more than enough of the world and the life that's out there –

Please allow me to ask you, Louise: will you be my wife?

LOUISE *sits frozen, without looking at him, her eyes full of tears*.

Don't give me an answer right away, but I'd like you to think it over. I'm not a young man any more, and you're not a naive young girl. But a friendship as old as ours has deep roots – and when all is said and done, perhaps twenty years of affection is a more solid foundation than a youthful infatuation.

LOUISE *shakes her head*.

I'm not talking about my feelings. I couldn't imagine any greater happiness on earth than being able to call you my wife, Miss Louise. And I would never ask for more than the right to provide the . . .

. . . the affection and support . . .

. . . that –

LOUISE. It won't ever be possible.

Mr MOLLER *gets up and starts to pace – dignified but highly emotional*.

MR MOLLER. Is it – (*With an effort.*) someone else?

LOUISE. Yes.

MR MOLLER. Then please accept my apologies.

But couldn't you have spared me this –

The POSTMAN *knocks, enters and holds up a letter.*

POSTMAN. For Miss Louise Strandberg!

Suddenly animated, LOUISE *runs up and takes the letter. The* POSTMAN *leaves.*

Afternoon!

LOUISE *hesitates with the letter in her hand.*

MR MOLLER. I hope I'm not in the way.

LOUISE. No, of course not – but if you don't mind . . .

She takes the letter to the window and starts reading. Her whole demeanour changes.

After a while:

MR MOLLER. I hope it brings good news.

LOUISE. Oh – you're still here! I'm sorry –

MR MOLLER. I can see it is good news.

LOUISE. Good or bad, time will tell.

MR MOLLER. So therein lies your cure.

LOUISE. Imagine if you had been walking, alone, for a long, long time, in utter darkness – and then, suddenly, there's a voice coming out of the gloom, and it's calling your name.

MR MOLLER. I sincerely hope that voice will not lead you astray.

I called your name, too.

He walks to the door.

LOUISE. I'm sorry. I'm very grateful to you. Sincerely.

I shall have to think things through, and then can I come and get some advice from you, before I leave?

MR MOLLER. You're leaving? When?

Where are you going?

LOUISE. Tomorrow or – in a few days, anyway. I'm going to Paris.

MR MOLLER. May God protect you on that journey.

Goodbye.

He exits.

LOUISE (*calling*). Botilda!

BOTILDA *hurries in.*

BOTILDA. That's more like it! You look a bit more cheerful now. He's proposed, hasn't he?

LOUISE. It's not that.

BOTILDA. Heavens above, what is it then?

LOUISE. Botilda – I'll be leaving in a few days time.

BOTILDA. Now then, what's all this? What are you up to? Where are you off to?

LOUISE. To Paris.

BOTILDA. You've gone completely mad! You can't do that!

LOUISE (*laughing*). I can!

BOTILDA. But you can't! You can't just go! What about the rain?

LOUISE. What *about* the rain?

BOTILDA. You can't go out on the sea when it's been raining like this for a fortnight! Just think how deep it'll be!

ACT FOUR

Paris. May the following year. LOUISE *enters from the bedroom in an elegant morning outfit. She paces aimlessly, checks the time, sits and dreams.*

ALLAND *enters quietly, watching her, then puts his hand on her head and bends her face to his.*

ALLAND. What do you think about, when you sit here all alone?

LOUISE. You, of course. You, you, you.

ALLAND. But what about me?

LOUISE. I think about you as the King of the Mountain Trolls. And I could sit here in my enchantment for a hundred years, and still it would feel as if only a few weeks had passed.

ALLAND. You almost alarm me.

LOUISE. Too much happiness?

ALLAND. Yes.

LOUISE *puts her hand over his mouth.*

LOUISE. Stop! I know what you're going to say.

ALLAND. But all things do have to end.

LOUISE. Don't think about it! '*La vie est belle*', remember?

ALLAND (*melancholic*). You are the most noble, the most lovely, the most wonderful woman . . .

LOUISE. I'm only a figment. I'm the result of a spell you cast.

ALLAND. I can see you in a fairy story, sitting at your spinning wheel, in some lovely gauzy dress. You'd be spinning silk, perhaps. You are as fine and delicate as the threads you spin – gossamer, almost. You might break at the slightest knock –

This might break you.

LOUISE. It doesn't matter now. At least I've had a bit of happiness.

ALLAND. But now you're going to be sensible, aren't you? You're going to forget, aren't you? All of this.

LOUISE. If you say so.

ALLAND. It'll be like having a single hair plucked out of your head – no worse than that.

LOUISE. So it is that time, is it? You're leaving, are you?

ALLAND. I've finished my sculpture, and the ship sails for New York tomorrow night. I did tell you. I've got a new commission waiting for me –

LOUISE. You told me, but I'd managed to forget.

ALLAND. Don't ruin it all by looking so tragical!

LOUISE. It can't be ruined. It's quite safe in my memory.

ALLAND. So you'll go back home?

LOUISE. Back to my cold, dark home?

ALLAND. Once you're there, you'll get back into the swing of things, I'm sure. Won't you? Come on, Lulu. You will. What is it? Lulu?

He's alarmed by the look on her face. She makes an effort to smile.

LOUISE. What is there to say? I love you.

ALLAND. No, no. We agreed not to talk about 'love'.

LOUISE. Haven't you realised? We may not have talked about it, but that's how it is for me. I couldn't have done it if I hadn't loved you. I couldn't have given myself to you just a little bit, just for a while.

ALLAND. I was afraid of this.

LOUISE. How tawdry that would be!

ALLAND. Not to me! There are plenty of women who –

LOUISE. No. It's not for me, that kind of love. I'd rather kill myself.

ALLAND. Lulu, how did it get to this? How could someone as pure and lovely as you get so attached to me? You've always known what I'm really like –

LOUISE. You're sensitive. Honest. And good. I adore you.

ALLAND. That's what they all say. Don't forget all of them.

LOUISE. Why should I care about them? This is what I feel.

ALLAND. You won't be the last, either. Bear that in mind. Show a bit of pride, for God's sake!

LOUISE. I shan't know anything about any of them. Shall I?

ALLAND. You're making this impossible for both of us.

LOUISE. I was trying to make it easy for you, since it's inevitable. Look – I can smile. I'm smiling to the bitter end. What else could you possibly wish for?

And I want to thank you, for – well, everything. No matter what happens.

And now, please go, if you must.

Kiss me here, and go.

She points to her forehead. He kisses her forehead, then her hand.

ALLAND. You're feverish. You're trembling.

LOUISE. No, no. I can be cool and calm, if that's what's required. Look. Cool and calm.

Don't forget me, Gustave.

Remember me as the one who would do anything to make you happy – even forget you, if that's what you wanted.

ALLAND (*moved, smiling in an attempt to hide his feelings*). I'll remember you as an idolater thinks of the best of his gods. I'll remember you as the one who was with me when I created my greatest work.

ERNA *opens the door, sees them and abruptly steps back.*

ERNA. I'm sorry –

ALLAND *turns to greet her.*

ALLAND. I was just leaving.

LOUISE. Are you really?

ALLAND. The private view is tonight. In a few hours time, the whole of Paris will be crowding into my studio, to say a lot of rubbish about my work. I suppose you should see it before they do.

LOUISE (*radiant*). May I?

ALLAND. Of course. But you'll have to be quick. The world will be upon us very soon.

LOUISE. I'll be there in half an hour.

ALLAND. I'll be waiting.

He kisses her hand and exits with a bow to ERNA, *who doesn't acknowledge him.*

ERNA. I won't keep you.

LOUISE. Are you all right, Erna? You look –

ERNA. You don't look so great yourself.

LOUISE. What's happened?

ERNA. Same old stuff. But today I couldn't stand it any longer. I told him to get packing.

LOUISE. Aren't you in love with him any more?

ERNA. In love with him? I've never been in love with him. How could you love someone like that? He's just a parasite, feeding off other people. He hasn't got anything of his own to contribute – no talent, no originality.

LOUISE. But you always knew that . . .

ERNA. Of course I knew it. He was better than nothing. I was broken-hearted, remember? Some women turn to the bottle.

I've never been much of a drinker. So I turned to other men, instead. It dulled the pain, for a while.

LOUISE. Oh God, Erna.

She strokes ERNA*'s cheek.*

ERNA. It was seeing them side by side that did it. The comparison was too stark. I'd supped with the gods, and there I was, slumming it with the dwarves.

Anyway, I'm going now.

LOUISE. Where?

ERNA. Out. Anywhere! I just need some air.

I can't stand his indifference to me! I want to compete on equal terms. I want to fight him like a man! I want to fight, and win. But it's not an equal fight. All I am now is his discarded lover. That's all he sees.

She collapses into a chair.

At a loss, LOUISE *puts her hand on* ERNA*'s head.*

LOUISE. Erna, I'm sorry. I've got to go out.

ERNA. I know. Go. Go on! I'll stay here – can I?

LOUISE. Of course – I won't be long.

If Viggo comes, tell him I'll be back soon. He's got some business to discuss with me.

LOUISE *exits. Some time passes.* ERNA *goes over to the bust of* ALLAND. *Suddenly vulnerable, she is about to touch it, when* VIGGO *enters. She immediately puts up her guard again.*

VIGGO. Hello! Is Louise here?

ERNA. She's with Alland. But she'll be back soon. What's up? You look a bit flustered.

VIGGO. I've had a bit of a shock, actually. I've received this letter, from Mr Moller back home. He's an old family friend, he looks after Louise's finances. He's always been totally scrupulous, and highly trusted. I don't know what to do, Erna.

Listen to this:

'It has not escaped my notice that considerable sums have been withdrawn from Miss Strandberg's account during the last few months. It seems unlikely to me that Miss Strandberg would be able to spend such large amounts herself. I would therefore ask you, with the utmost discretion, and purely out of concern for your stepsister, to attempt to shed some light on the matter. For reasons of some delicacy, I would find it difficult to discuss these matters with her myself. Please be assured that I would not trouble you with this if the situation were not already cause for grave concern. Miss Strandberg has almost completely exhausted her financial resources.'

ERNA. It doesn't surprise me. You can't live like a duchess in Paris without paying for it through the nose.

VIGGO. I think she must have paid for the studio with her own money.

ERNA. The stingy dog! This all adds up to a very expensive indulgence for a poor, lonely, country girl with a paltry few thousand in the bank.

VIGGO. Poor old Lou!

ERNA. No. It's the best thing that could have happened. Now she'll be forced to face up to it. She'll have to go home.

VIGGO. She must have some money in reserve.

ERNA. You should write to the bank manager and tell him to put a stop on all future requests for funds.

VIGGO. No. I can't.

ERNA. She's completely lost her head. We have to take responsibility for her, or she'll destitute herself.

VIGGO. No, Erna, we can't act against her wishes.

ERNA. Well, you can't stop me trying to knock some sense into her. I won't just stand here like a post and say nothing.

A carriage is heard pulling up outside.

VIGGO. Do what you can. Tell her the whole story, if you like. But remember how stubborn she is.

ERNA. I'll talk to her. But I'd like to be alone with her.

VIGGO. All right. I'll be in the garden.

He exits to the garden.

LOUISE *enters. She is pale and staring, like a sleepwalker.*

ERNA. What is it? What's happened now?

LOUISE. Nothing.

ERNA. Are you all right?

LOUISE. Yes! I'm fine.

ERNA. Don't fib. Something's happened with Alland.

LOUISE. I've just been to his studio. I've seen his new piece. Everyone agrees that it's his most outstanding work yet.

ERNA. So why has it made you like this?

LOUISE. He calls it 'Fate'. It's a group.

ERNA. Fate! What's that supposed to mean?

LOUISE. I was the first to arrive – that's what he wanted. He pulled off the tarpaulin, and –

ERNA. What?

LOUISE. I'll never forget it. The marble, dazzling white . . .

ERNA. Was it you?

LOUISE. Fate, that's what he's called it –

ERNA. And the figures? There are figures? You said it was a group.

LOUISE. The central figure is a woman – huge, larger than life size, her eyes fixed on something ahead of her. And she has trampled over a body, which is thrown aside, and lies crushed on the ground.

ERNA. The body of another woman?

LOUISE. Yes. A powerless, naked body, lifeless but exquisite – and the face! She has an expression of tranquillity, of release . . . She is serenely oblivious to mortal suffering. It's the work of a genius, it's prophetic –

ERNA. Calm down, Louise.

LOUISE. He's a great, great man, and I've treated him as an equal! I've been presumptuous enough to believe that he needed some comfort that I had to offer, and yet he is –

ERNA. He's thoroughly human. Just like you. Just like me.

LOUISE. No. I don't think you truly know him – I don't think I knew him, until today. Until I saw the greatness of his work.

ERNA. I'm sure he very much enjoyed watching this Damascene moment of yours.

LOUISE. It was like being confronted with something more than human. Something sublime. The dead woman has my features, you see, but she is nobler, immortal, preserved for eternity –

ERNA. Don't take it too hard, Louise.

LOUISE. The figure of Fate – the unshakable destiny. Everything must yield before Fate, or be crushed. Fate rolls over human life –

ERNA. Louise, I think you should lie down. I think you should calm down.

LOUISE *sinks down into a chair.*

LOUISE. Yes.

It's over. That was his way of saying goodbye.

ERNA. The louse.

LOUISE (*vehemently*). Don't say that! You've got no right! He hasn't betrayed me, or you, or anyone! He's just different from the rest of us. He's different.

ERNA. He's a bastard. And now, at last, you are going to close your door to him, and refuse to let him in.

LOUISE. Me? Refuse him?

ERNA. Yes! You owe it to yourself.

LOUISE. I'm not proud.

ERNA. Then you should be. It's time to go back home, Louise!

LOUISE. Home? I have no home.

ERNA. Listen to me. Listen. You just can't afford to stay here any longer. I mean financially. You don't work, you don't have any income, you're just spending money. And Louise, are you listening? It seems that Viggo has had a letter from your bank manager –

LOUISE. Don't talk to me about this now. I'm too tired.

ERNA. It's important. You've got to understand that your finances –

LOUISE. Leave me alone, Erna. Go!

ERNA. I see.

ERNA *heads angrily for the door*.

I'm going.

LOUISE *pulls her back*.

LOUISE. Erna, at least say goodbye before you go. My sweet Erna! Don't be angry. You've been a good friend to me, I know.

Now, please, go home.

She bundles ERNA *out of the door. It's now dark. She lights the lamp and sits at the table.*

The day of reckoning has come. *Qu'est-ce qu'elle est belle, la vie!* It seems hard to leave it.

She writes. After a while, VIGGO *enters from the garden.*

VIGGO. Am I intruding?

LOUISE folds what she is writing and covers it with the blotter.

LOUISE. Not at all. I'm glad you're here.

VIGGO. Has Erna gone?

LOUISE. Just, yes. I wasn't very nice to her, I'm afraid.

VIGGO. She was in a very peculiar state. Do you know why?

LOUISE. She's left Henrik.

VIGGO. Poor Erna!

LOUISE. If she'd really loved him, she wouldn't have been so anguished about it. If you truly love someone, even though that love ruins you, even though it brings poverty and loneliness, it still makes you happy. But if you do all of that for someone you don't even love –

VIGGO. And for such a gifted and sensitive person like her to live like that –

LOUISE. Don't judge her too harshly. She's suffered terribly.

VIGGO. I'm not judging anyone.

LOUISE. No. You're such a good person. Can you stay with me for a little while?

VIGGO. Yes.

LOUISE. I feel so strange! On one hand I feel so helpless, so sad! But at the same time I feel exhilarated.

VIGGO. Maybe I should ask Erna to come down?

LOUISE. No! I only want you. We were always together as children. I want it to be like that again.

VIGGO. Louise, you're really not well.

LOUISE. Don't worry. I'll take myself off to sleep in a minute.

VIGGO. Good.

LOUISE. Wait just a moment, though. Come and look.

She goes into the garden. VIGGO follows.

Can you smell that lilac? And look at the stars, just starting to come out. God's making tiny holes with a pin, giving us poor humans a little glimpse of the wonders of heaven.

Do you believe in heaven?

Maybe there's nothing behind that dark blue veil.

Maybe there's just a huge fire, and every evening all we're seeing is showers of sparks falling down through the roof of our world. When I was a little girl I was always terrified that one night the whole sky would catch fire, and that great inferno up there would come crashing down on our heads and burn us all to ash.

VIGGO. Come on. Inside! You're running a fever and you'll catch a chill out here.

He brings her in and closes the door.

LOUISE. I haven't looked at the stars like that since I was a child. It's as if I haven't seen them, all these years. It's as if they're lost to you, as an adult. The sky is so immense, so black, it makes you shrink into insignificance. We're dust, that's all. We think we know about joy and sorrow, but that's as nothing.

VIGGO. Time for bed, Louise.

LOUISE. Imagine if the sky started to grow, bigger and bigger, closer and closer until we were all engulfed –

VIGGO *takes her arm.*

VIGGO. Louise!

LOUISE. Yes, yes, Viggo. I'm going.

She heads for the bedroom, then stops.

But there's so much to say, so much to talk about.

She sits, and smiles at him.

You're engaged to be married, Viggo.

VIGGO. Yes.

LOUISE. And will you go back home, then? Get a job with a newspaper, then start a family? Will you live with Lilly for ever and ever?

VIGGO. I suppose so – yes.

LOUISE. Does that thought make you happy?

VIGGO. Yes – but . . .

LOUISE. And Lilly will be Mrs Pihl.

VIGGO. Yes.

LOUISE. She'll put flowers in vases in the rooms, and care for you, and make you happy.

VIGGO. Yes, Louise, but –

LOUISE *nods*.

LOUISE. Good. Free love is just for trolls, not for humans. 'Look out for yourself, and no one else,' they say. But it doesn't suit us humans.

VIGGO *brushes her hair away from her face and tries to lie her down on the chaise longue.*

VIGGO. Hush now. No more words.

LOUISE. No – I'm off to bed now. If you sit at the table, you'll hear me if I call.

VIGGO. Yes, but I think I ought to call Erna –

LOUISE. No, no. All I need is a good, long sleep. If I don't call for you, you'll know I'm peaceful. I think that's best, don't you?

VIGGO. Sleep well, then.

LOUISE. How long will you stay, do you think?

VIGGO. The whole night, if you want me to.

LOUISE *embraces him.*

LOUISE. Thank you, thank you, you loyal soul.

She goes into the bedroom. He sits at the table. She returns.

If anyone calls – I mean, if Alland calls –

VIGGO. What?

LOUISE. Don't disturb me. I'm too tired.

She goes to her room.

VIGGO *sits down to read, but soon casts the book aside, gets up and rings the bell.*

CONCIERGE (*from the hall*). What is it? What's the matter – ringing at this time of night?

VIGGO. Could you get a message to Mademoiselle Wallden, please. She has a studio on the top floor.

CONCIERGE. No, I cannot!

VIGGO. I can't go myself, I daren't leave – but I'll pay two francs for the message to be delivered. Here.

CONCIERGE. What's the message, then?

VIGGO. Just ask Mademoiselle Wallden to please come down.

CONCIERGE. Very well.

She takes the money.

VIGGO. But please, hurry.

CONCIERGE *exits.*

VIGGO *tries to sit quietly, but is anxious.*

ALLAND *enters, and stops at the door. He is in evening dress, and someone has put a laurel wreath around his head.*

VIGGO *signals for him to be quiet.*

Louise is not well.

ALLAND. Is she in bed?

VIGGO. Yes.

ALLAND. So why . . . What are you doing here?

VIGGO. I promised I'd stay.

ALLAND. I must talk to her. I've decided not to leave.

VIGGO. I'm sorry. You can't see her.

ALLAND. I was rather concerned when she left me. She was – she seemed . . .

VIGGO. Yes. That's why she needs to rest. That's why I'm staying here, to watch over her.

ALLAND. I couldn't get away when she left – but I'm here, now. I'm going to stay.

VIGGO. As you please.

ALLAND. Can I take your place, Monsieur?

VIGGO. No. No, you can't take my place. I'm sorry.

ALLAND. But I have to talk to her. It's important.

What was that?

VIGGO. I didn't hear anything.

ERNA *enters hurriedly from the hall.*

ERNA. What's going on?

VIGGO. Louise has fallen ill again. I didn't want to be here on my own – I think she might need you.

ERNA *tiptoes up to the bedroom door and listens.*

VIGGO. Don't wake her if she's asleep.

ERNA (*looking through the keyhole*). The light's out. Everything seems quiet.

VIGGO. Then she must be asleep. What's this?

He has accidentally pushed aside the blotting paper which was hiding the note LOUISE *was writing. He picks it up.*

(*To* ALLAND.) It's addressed to you.

ALLAND *takes the letter out of his hand and reads. Then he drops the letter and rushes to the bedroom door.*

ALLAND. Louise!

VIGGO (*blocking the way*). What is it?

ALLAND *pushes him aside, opens the door and rushes into the bedroom.*

ALLAND. Bring some light.

VIGGO *takes a lamp. He and* ERNA *go to the door. They see that* LOUISE *is not there.*

VIGGO (*bemused*). Where is she?

ALLAND *runs out of the bedroom and exits from the studio.* VIGGO *grabs the letter that* ALLAND *has dropped, and reads.*

ERNA. What does it say?

VIGGO *hands the letter to* ERNA. *Outside, shouts are heard, rising in volume.* VIGGO *goes to the window to look.*

VIGGO (*calling outside*). What's happened? What's happened?

HENRIK *stumbles into the room, pale and terrified.*

HENRIK. I saw her. I was down by the river, but I couldn't stop her –

I'm sorry. I'm so sorry.

ALLAND *enters, carrying* LOUISE'*s dead body, wet with river water.*

VIGGO *and* ERNA *go to her. They take the body and try to rouse her.*

VIGGO. Louise?

ALLAND. No.

ERNA (*to* LOUISE, *stroking her head*). You did it. Oh God, you did it.

VIGGO *and* ERNA *lie her on the chaise longue.* ALLAND *stumbles backwards, head bowed.*

VIGGO *and* ERNA *attend to the body.* ERNA *cries in anger and sorrow.*

HENRIK. Erna, please . . .

HENRIK *goes to* ERNA, *attempts to put his arms around her. She angrily shrugs him off. She stands and looks at* ALLAND.

ERNA (*to* ALLAND). Look. Look what you've done.

ALLAND *quietly exits.*